ONCE AGAIN IN PUBLIC

The Witches' Almanac

SPRING 2003 — SPRING 2004

For the first time combining the mysterious wiccan and arcane
secrets of an old England witch with one from New England

Prepared and edited by
ELIZABETH PEPPER and JOHN WILCOCK

CONTAINING pictorial and explicit delineations of the magical phases of
the Moon together with full and complete information about astrological
portents of the year to come and various aspects of occult knowledge
enabling all who read to improve their lives in the old manner.

The Witches' Almanac, Ltd.

Publishers   Newport

Address all inquiries and information to
THE WITCHES' ALMANAC, LTD.
P.O. Box 289
Tiverton, Rhode Island 02878-0289

COPYRIGHT 2003 BY THE WITCHES' ALMANAC, LTD.
All rights reserved.

ISBN: 1-881098-22-2

ISSN: 1522-3183

First Printing January 2003

Printed in the United States of America

Preface

Luck is such a light and fleeting thing that the word itself almost defies definition. "That which happens to one seemingly by chance," as supplied by dictionaries, fails to capture the magic and wonder of mysterious happenstance. Fate and destiny assume meanings of solemn inevitability, but good luck is a kind of random delight. Everybody knows the exhilaration that unexpected good fortune brings. And as there seems to be no rhyme or reason for it, most people tend to accept fortune's benefits without question. The craft views the gifts of chance with different eyes.

Imagine luck as an unseen force whirling around the world with as much potential for good as for ill. Acknowledge its presence and seek to understand its nature as it pertains to you. Learn by experience to recognize particular areas of endeavor where your personal good fortune prevails. Accept change as the essence of existence, for whatever proved unfavorable in the past may very well shift as time goes by. An initial setback may clear the path for an ultimate triumph. Awareness of the positive and negative factors of life, as well as correct attitude, create its form. In the quest to repel evil and attract good favor, the surest guide is often your inner voice. And above all, maintain hope, courage, and confidence, for these are qualities irresistible to that fickle creature known as Lady Luck.

HOLIDAYS

Spring 2003 to Spring 2004

March 20	Vernal Equinox
April 1	All Fools' Day
April 30	Beltane Eve
May 1	Roodmas
May 8	White Lotus Day
May 9, 11, 13	Lemuria
May 29	Oak Apple Day
June 5	Night of the Watchers
June 20	Midsummer Night
June 21	Summer Solstice
June 24	St. John's Day
July 31	Lughnassad Eve
August 1	Lammas
August 13	Diana's Day
August 29	Day of Thoth
September 23	Autumnal Equinox
October 31	Samhain Eve
November 1	Hallowmas
November 16	Hecate Night
December 17	Saturnalia
December 21	Winter Solstice
January 9	Feast of Janus
February 1	Oimelc Eve
February 2	Candlemas
March 1	Matronalia

CONTENTS

Today and Tomorrow 6
Full Moon Names 10
The Way of the Moon 11
Year of the Ram 12
The Moon Calendar 13
East Wind, West Wind 14
Long ago and far away 16
The Magician 18
Sound Advice 20
The Hazel Tree 22
Death and the Maiden 24
The Mystery of Venus de Milo 26
Masquerade 28
Negative Confession 30
A friend in need 32
The Wolf and the Crane 34
Winds of the Rede 36
Finding the Aradia Papers 39
Fairy Gifts 40
What is your PSI potential? 44
Presage 45
Astrological Keys 46
Nighttime People in a Daytime World .. 72
Ghosts of the Dry Tortugas 74
Horses of Myth 76
Window on the Weather 77
Music of the Spheres 82
The Owl 84
Mercury 86
Moon Gardening 88
Names 89

ELIZABETH PEPPER & JOHN WILCOCK
Executive Editors

KERRY CUDMORE
Managing Editor

BARBARA STACY
JEAN MARIE WALSH
Associate Editors

Astrologer — Dikki-Jo Mullen
Climatologist — Tom C. Lang
Consulting Editor — Margaret Adams
Production — Bendigo Associates
Research — Susan Chaunt
Sales — Ellen Lynch

FOUR WINDS

"FOUR winds blowing through the sky,
You have seen poor maidens die,
Tell me then what I shall do
That my lover may be true."
Said the wind from out the south,
"Lay no kiss upon his mouth,"
And the wind from out the west,
"Wound the heart within his breast,"
And the wind from out the east,
"Send him empty from the feast,"
And the wind from out the north,
"In the tempest thrust him forth;
When thou art more cruel than he,
Then will Love be kind to thee."

— SARA TEASDALE

today and tomorrow

By Oliver Johnson

HIGH PRIESTESSES? Speculation that the priestesses of ancient Delphi intoned their pronouncements while intoxicated seem to have been confirmed recently. Tests have proven the existence of methane, ethane, and ethylene in the Delphi rocks and in the waters of a nearby spring. The startling conclusion derives from John Hale, an archaeologist at the University of Louisville, and Jelle Zeilings de Boer, a geologist at Wesleyan University. "The findings," according to Geology magazine, "challenged a century of research which had maintained that the priests and the oracle were deceiving the public and inventing stories to boost the site's importance."

According to Plutarch, the oracle delivered her ambiguous pronouncements perched on a three-legged stool in an underground chamber murky with gases. The site's importance hardly needed boosting, for Delphi was enormously influential. Kings and emperors visited the oracle as well as ordinary people who craved to know what the future held. Croesus, king of Lydia, declared war on Cyrus of Persia after the oracle told him that "a great nation would fall" if he crossed the Halys River. Unfortunately the great nation proved to be his own. On another drastic occasion, after the Trojan War Orestes was given the go-ahead to seek vengeance on his mother for murdering his father, Agamemnon.

Today the gases no longer penetrate the oracular sanctuary. But according to toxicologist Henry Spiller of the Delphi research team, ethylene is "a great gas," at one time widely used as an anaesthetic. Its onset is rapid and in low doses produces "disembodied euphoria with periods of excitation and amnesia."

GINNER
Old Icelandic symbol for divine, demonical

CAUTION, ELF CROSSING. Erla Stefansdottir frequently gets calls from prospective homeowners in Iceland (pop. 275,000) wanting to make sure that their new houses are free of spirits. In a country where belief in "hidden folk" prevails, Stefansdottir is Iceland's most famous "elf spotter." Occasionally she arbitrates disputes between the Public Roads Administration and locals worried that construction crews will demolish hallowed boulders – and with them the invisible homes of their invisible occupants. The agency often defers to her wisdom, rerouting a road or delaying construction and chalking it up to public relations. According to an agency spokesperson, "When Native Americans protest roads being built over ancient burial grounds, the U.S. listens. It's the same here. There are people who believe in elves and we don't make fun of them. We try to deal with them."

WHERE'S THE LECHE? Noting that milk consumption by teenagers has dropped by 12%, the Milk Board reached into mythology to target Hispanic consumption. The ghostly pitchwoman in the commercial stars La Lorona, "the crying one," who appears in translucent form floating through a deserted house to the refrigerator. It contains only an empty carton. "Got milk?" spoken in English, is the only dialogue. Results of the imaginative ad campaign have not been released, but the spoilsport Wall Street Journal predicts that "broadcasting the spot on English-language TV risks alienating Anglos who are unfamiliar with the ghost."

WATER, WATER EVERYWHERE. For more than 35 years, octogenarian Bill Cox has wandered over barren hills and dales finding water with a flexible steel rod he calls an aurameter. He says he feels, sees, hears and tastes the water long before the digging starts. Cox has an impressive record of success in Canada, Japan, Egypt, Brazil and the American Southwest. He has written nine books and lectures worldwide. The mysterious skill has adherents of all ages, and the American Society of Dowsers in Danville, Vermont, has more than four thousand members. Cox, who often waives his $600 fee, says his favorite jobs are "lost causes," where no one else has been able to find water. Origins of the "water witch" go back hundreds of years. Their efforts are dismissed by hydrologists and geologists, who claim that there is nothing scientific in dowsing. But Cox's successes defy objective skepticism. He even has a monument to his accomplishments on Awaji Island in Japan. Hired by an initially doubtful Jitso Tanagi, Cox easily located a new well. Says Tanagi, "Through Mr. Cox we have become reacquainted with the bountifulness of nature and learned of the wonderful potential of the human senses."

KITE POWER. Apparently far-fetched theories that the ancient Egyptians might have used wind power to erect the pyramids arose when a team from the California Institute of Technology lifted a three-ton obelisk by flying a nylon parasail into a 16 mph wind. According to project leader Emilio Castano Graff, "This doesn't prove the Egyptians used kites to build the pyramids, but it shows that it is possible to use the energy of the winds to lift heavy objects." Archaeologists are skeptical. "There are no indications that they used kites," responds UCLA professor Willeke Wendrich. "We have no depictions. We don't even have words in Egyptian for kite." Tomb drawings and other artifacts, she added, only point to ramps, levers and other techniques.

Zulu prayer mat, Republic of South Africa

HEALING PRACTITIONER. South African *sangomas*, traditional healers, are lobbying Parliament to recognize their profession so that patients can pay for treatments with medical insurance. An estimated 200,000 *sangomas* practice here, offering consultations from $2 to $10 exclusive of medications. Few practitioners are Caucasian, but Janine Andrews, 31, is an exception. She operates in the scenic Valley of a Thousand Hills region near Howick. Patients begin treatments sitting on an animal-skin mat as the sacred herb *mpepho* is burned to cleanse the atmosphere. Even as a child, Janine was drawn to healing in ancient ways. "I wanted to learn about traditional herbs," she says. "I was always a lover of mystery, of drumming and culture. I was kind of searching for a place to belong. I was searching for something deeper that I couldn't find in my own culture, and this is where I found it."

ALL CREATURES GREAT AND SMALL. Since Chicago installed a herd of fiberglass cows on its streets years ago some cities have been copy cats. Naturally variations occurred. Cincinnati went in for plastic pigs. Orlando, Florida, opted for alligators. Santa Catalina, California, chose buffalo for their historical connection. The island still hosts a herd remaining from filming a Zane Grey novel in the thirties. But now Thousand Oaks, California, has broken new ground by populating the streets with five-foot rabbits. "It gives us a symbol; it says we are a valley of peace and contentment," explains mayor Ed Masry. "Who hates rabbits? I don't know anyone who is a rabbit hater." Delighted locals see the project as a return to the area's rabbity roots. Thousand Oaks is situated in the Conero Valley, and *conejo* is the Spanish word for rabbit.

Also in the news is the inscrutable owl, which found itself in demand following release of the first Harry Potter film. But don't try getting one. Owls are protected under international treaties and federal laws which ban keeping them as pets to prevent their dwindling to an endangered species. Eastern Siberian owls, for example, are so rare that only 200 pairs are known to exist. Not so the common barn owl, on which farmers rely to keep down the gopher population. Some people love gophers too, but the underground dwellers do extensive damage by destroying crops and feasting on tree roots. The gopher-hunting owl can see in the dark from several hundred feet, has hollow bones and feathers so light it can soar in total silence. "It's like a ghost flying by," avers Tom Hoffman, who owns a vineyard in the San Joaquin Valley.

Another creature occasionally heard but seldom seen is the loveable little pine marten, a secretive relative of the stoat or weasel with nocturnal habits so quiet naturalists believed it might be extinct. But Johnny Bates, spokesman for the London-based Vincent Wildlife Trust, initiated an extensive search for the elusive creature and came up with good news. "We are encouraged by a constant pattern of reports," says Bates.

IN BRIEF. The annual Valentine's Day adults-only sex tour of the San Francisco Zoo, now in its fourteenth year, is always sold out. Visitors don't actually get to see animals doing the deed, but they hear all about their mating habits from a tour guide on the $50 trolley ride past all the exhibits.... Dr. John Shepard of the Mayo Clinic's Sleep Disorder Center studied 300 pet owners and discovered that almost half slept with their pets. A substantial number of these bedmates were habitually awakened by the snoring of their dog or cat....Oxford University researchers have discovered a crow that bent wire into a hook to pull up a bucket of food out of reach. "Betty may be a crow, but she's no bird brain," reported the Associated Press story.

The Pine Marten by Thomas Bewick, c. 1800

FULL MOON NAMES

Students of occult literature soon learn the importance of names. From Ra to Rumpelstiltskin, the message is clear—names hold unusual power.

The tradition of naming full Moons was recorded in an English edition of *The Shepherd's Calendar*, published in the first decade of the 16th century.

Aries - Seed. Sowing season and symbol of the start of the new year.
Taurus - Hare. The sacred animal was associated in Roman legends with springtime and fertility.
Gemini - Dyad. The Latin word for a pair refers to the twin stars of the constellation Castor and Pollux.
Cancer - Mead. During late June and most of July the meadows, or meads, were mowed for hay.
Leo - Wort. When the sun was in Leo the worts (from the Anglo-Saxon *wyrt-*plant) were gathered to be dried and stored.
Virgo - Barley. Persephone, virgin goddess of rebirth, carries a sheaf of barley as symbol of the harvest.
Libra - Blood. Marking the season when domestic animals were sacrificed for winter provisions.
Scorpio - Snow. Scorpio heralds the dark season when the Sun is at its lowest and the first snow flies.
Sagittarius - Oak. The sacred tree of the Druids and the Roman god Jupiter is most noble as it withstands winter's blasts.
Capricorn - Wolf. The fearsome nocturnal animal represents the "night" of the year. Wolves were rarely seen in England after the 12th century.
Aquarius - Storm. A storm is said to rage most fiercely just before it ends, and the year usually follows suit.
Pisces - Chaste. The antiquated word for pure reflects the custom of greeting the new year with a clear soul.

Libra's Full Moon occasionally became the Wine Moon when a grape harvest was expected to produce a superior vintage.

America's early settlers continued to name the full Moons. The influence of the native tribes and their traditions is readily apparent.

AMERICAN	Colonial	Native
Aries / April	Pink, Grass, Egg	Green Grass
Taurus / May	Flower, Planting	Shed
Gemini / June	Rose, Strawberry	Rose, Make Fat
Cancer / July	Buck, Thunder	Thunder
Leo / August	Sturgeon, Grain	Cherries Ripen
Virgo / September	Harvest, Fruit	Hunting
Libra / October	Hunter's	Falling Leaf
Scorpio / November	Beaver, Frosty	Mad
Sagittarius / December	Cold, Long Night	Long Night
Capricorn / January	Wolf, After Yule	Snow
Aquarius / February	Snow, Hunger	Hunger
Pisces / March	Worm, Sap, Crow	Crow, Sore Eye

THE WAY OF THE MOON

A New Moon rises with the Sun,
Her waxing half at midday shows,
The Full Moon climbs at sunset hour,
And waning half the midnight knows.

NEW 2004	**FULL**	**NEW** 2005	**FULL**
January 21	January 7	January 10	January 25
February 20	February 6	February 8	February 23
March 20	March 6	March 10	March 25
April 19	April 5	April 8	April 24
May 18	May 4	May 8	May 23
June 17	June 3	June 6	June 21
July 17	July 2/31	July 6	July 21
August 15	August 29	August 4	August 19
September 14	September 28	September 3	September 17
October 13	October 27	October 3	October 17
November 12	November 26	November 1	November 16
December 11	December 26	December 1/30	December 15

Life takes on added dimension when you match your activities to the waxing and waning of the Moon. Observe the sequence of her phases to learn the wisdom of constant change within complete certainty.

YEAR OF THE RAM
February 1, 2003 to January 21, 2004

Unlike the West's formidable Ram of Aries, the Orient's counterpart is a gentle herd animal. Its astrological meaning is quiet joy and bliss. We may look forward to a year marked by compassion and moderation. Expect a certain amount of fluctuation in political and financial quarters, but keep hope alive. Just as things appear to be close to disaster, something unexpected occurs to save the day. Enjoy the slow pace and harmony inherent in a Ram Year.

Oriental astrological years run in cycles of twelve, each governed by a symbolic creature. If you were born on or after the New Moon in the sign of Aquarius during the following years, welcome a surge of creativity and trust your imagination.

1907   1919   1931   1943   1955   1967   1979   1991   2003

The MOON Calendar

 is divided into zodiac signs rather than the more familiar Gregorian calendar.

2003   2004

 Bear in mind that new projects should be initiated when the Moon is waxing (from dark to full); when the Moon is on the wane (from full to dark), it is a time for storing energy and the wise person waits.

Please note that Moons are listed by day of entry into each sign. Quarters are marked, but as rising and setting times vary from one region to another, it is advisable to check your local newspaper, library or planetarium.

The Moon's Place is computed for Eastern Standard Time.

East Wind, West Wind

From the east comes the veering wind, the one which blows in the same direction as the sun's passage across the sky. A veering wind is purifying. When you feel confused and out of sorts, there is no more effective remedy than a taste of the east wind. Make a ceremony of it. Go to the highest and least obstructed place you know and stand very still facing into the wind. Don't brace yourself against it. Let it flow through you, sweeping away any problems blocking your peace of mind. Ask for the clarity of heart and soul it can give. When you are not clear yourself, you will be of no use to anyone else.

The west wind is called the backing wind because it moves against the course of the sun. It's a supporting wind, one to erase negativity and renew confidence. This is the wind to walk in; to walk at the wind's will. It's a delicious feeling to be borne along by its force. The poet Shelley in his *Ode to the West Wind* wrote, "Drive my dead thoughts over the universe like withered leaves to quicken a new birth!" The familiar Irish salutation: "May the wind be always at your back" is possibly a folk memory of this simple rite.

Blending ritual and nature is a vital key to psychic well-being. By drawing strength and comfort from the veering and backing winds, we prepare ourselves for the work we must do.

 **aries** March 21- April 20

Mars   Cardinal Sign of Fire

s	m	t	w	t	f	s
					Mar. **21** Take your time Scorpio	**22** Plan your garden Sagittarius
				2003 Vernal Equinox		
23 A green wind sings	**24** ◐ Capricorn	**25**	**26** Vesta beckons now	**27** Take no chances Aquarius	**28** Smile, laugh, play	**29** Pisces
30 Walk in the woods	**31** Shift a pattern	April **1** ● All Fools' Aries	**2** WAXING Mercury is bright	**3** Learn something new Taurus	**4** Plant root crops	**5** Start a journal
6 Daylight Saving 2 a.m. Gemini	**7** Jackie Chan born, 1954	**8** Think clearly Cancer	**9** ◑	**10** Leo	**11** Till the soil	**12** Consult the Tarot
13 Forgive a wrong Virgo	**14** Banish malice	**15** Plant flowers tomorrow Libra	**16** seed moon	**17** WANING Scorpio	**18**	**19** Kate Hudson born, 1979 Sagittarius
20 Enjoy repose						

Long ago and far away

Gothic England and Scotland knew the May Day feast as Roodmas, or Rood Day. The theme of the holiday was joyful anticipation: time set apart to delight the senses with the promise of summer. Homes were decorated with greenery and spring blossoms. Baskets filled with treats were secretly delivered to a loved one before dawn. A branch of elder cut with solemn ceremony on the last day of April was tied with bright red ribbons and hung above the hearth. Traditional music charmed the ear. The warm sweet smell of Roodmas baking made an unforgettable memory.

ROODMAS SUN WAFERS

1/2 cup (1 stick) butter, at room temperature
1 cup sugar
1 egg, warm to the touch
A dash of salt
1 cup sifted all-purpose flour
3 teaspoons flavoring (brandy, vanilla, or almond extract)
White of egg

Cream together the butter and sugar in a large mixing bowl. Add the egg, slightly beaten. Gradually combine the salt, flour, and flavoring. Mix well. Cover the bowl and chill the dough for three hours.

Preheat the oven to 375 degrees. With floured fingers, shape the dough into small balls and place them on lightly greased cookie sheets. Figure about 36 wafers in all. Flatten each ball with the heel of your palm and lightly brush with white of egg. Bake for about 13 minutes, or until the edges are brown and look like the tiny golden suns they represent.

♉ taurus — April 21- May 21

Venus — *Fixed Sign of Earth*

S	M	T	W	T	F	S
	April 21 *Delay all action* Capricorn	22	23 Aquarius	24 *Greet the dawn*	25 *Avoid gossips* Pisces	26 *Do not gamble*
27 *Prepare for the feast*	28 Floralia Aries	29 *Patience pays off*	30 Roodmas Eve Taurus	May 1 BELTANE	2 WAXING	3 *Fortune smiles* Gemini
4 *Renew psychic energy*	5 Cancer	6 *Make a new friend*	7 *Serve a cause*	8 White Lotus Day Leo	9 Lemuria begins	10 *Draw a symbol* Virgo
11 Natasha Richardson born, 1963	12 Libra	13 *Work a spell*	14 *Prepare for the eclipse* Scorpio	15 hare moon Total lunar eclipse	16 WANING Sagittarius	17 *Lose not substance for shadow*
18 *Carry a charm* Capricorn	19 *Create an illusion*	20 Aquarius	21 Albrecht Dürer born, 1471			

THE MAGICIAN

The Magician, from the Rider pack created by A. E. Waite and drawn by Pamela Coleman Smith in 1910.

Early French packs of the Tarot's Major Arcana titled the Number I card *Le Bateleur*, The Juggler. Magician and Juggler imply skill, dexterity, one who performs tricks. Such attributes belong to Hermes/Mercury — the classical god of invention, eloquence, cleverness and luck. The Messenger God's mythic role is guide and conductor of souls.

A lemniscate, the horizontal figure eight representing eternal life, is the ancient symbol ascribed to Hermes. In mathematics, it denotes infinity. The cosmic emblem is clearly displayed in the Rider deck shown above. The symbol may often be found in other Tarot decks, artfully decorating the Magician's broad-brimmed hat.

He faces a table upon which rest tokens of the Minor Arcana's four suits: Wands (Fire), Coins (Earth), Swords (Air) and Cups (Water). The Magician's unifying gesture draws power from above to achieve earthly manifestation.

The card suggests that humankind may possess a potential ability to shape destiny. Self-confidence, initiative, and a strong will are factors in reaching a goal. Understand yourself and the four elements governing chance to aid in claiming success and the ultimate fulfillment of desire.

♊ gemini — May 22 – June 21
Mercury — *Mutable Sign of Air*

S	M	T	W	T	F	S
				May 22 ◐ Pisces	23 *Avoid a blunder*	24
25 Emerson born, 1803 Aries	26 *Retrace your steps*	27 Taurus	28 *The lost is found*	29 Oak Apple Day	30 ● Gemini	31 *Do it yourself*
June 1 WAXING	2 *Tackle a new project* Cancer	3 *Wake up singing*	4 Leo	5 Watchers' Night	6 *Erase doubts* Virgo	7 ◑
8 *Comfort a friend*	9 Libra	10 *Accept a compliment*	11 *Cancel a debt* Scorpio	12 *Try harder*	13 *Draw down the Moon* Sagittarius	14 dyad moon
15 WANING Capricorn	16 *Heed a message in the wind*	17 Venus Williams born, 1980 Aquarius	18	19 *Find Mars at midnight* Pisces	20 Midsummer Eve SUMMER SOLSTICE ☞	21 ◐ Aries

19

SOUND ADVICE

Witches are often called upon to give advice. Here are a few words of wisdom to pass along:

Whatever your advice, make it brief.
— HORACE

Many receive advice, few profit by it.
— PUBLILIUS SYRUS

The best and surest method of advice should spare the person, though it brands the vice.
— ROBERT BURTON

Hold faithfulness and sincerity as first principles.
— CONFUCIUS

Be ever soft and pliable like a reed, not hard and unbending like a cedar.
— THE TALMUD

It is better to receive than to inflict an injury.
— CICERO

Learn to limit yourself, to content yourself with some definite thing, and some definite work; dare to be what you are, and learn to resign with a good grace all that you are not, and to believe in your own individuality.
— HENRI-FRÉDÉRIC AMIEL

Self-control is the quality that distinguishes the fittest to survive.
— GEORGE BERNARD SHAW

Never be mean in anything; never be false; never be cruel. Avoid those three vices,...and I can always be hopeful of you. (Aunt Betsey Trotwood to David in David Copperfield.)
— CHARLES DICKENS

This above all, — to thine ownself be true; and it must follow, as the night the day, thou canst not then be false to any man. (Polonius to Laertes in Hamlet.)
— SHAKESPEARE

In giving advice seek to help, not to please, your friend.
— SOLON

Life is a privilege and a challenge. Endeavor to be as perfect as you can.
— SAMUEL JOHNSON

(Famed maxims carved on a column in the temple to Apollo at Delphi.)
Know thyself and *Nothing in excess.*

 **cancer** June 22- July 23

Moon *Cardinal Sign of Water*

s	m	T	W	T	F	s
June 22 *Locate wild herbs*	23 *Empress Josephine born, 1763*	24 *St. John's Day* Taurus	25	26 *Maintain a sense of humor* Gemini	27 *Keep a clear head*	28 *Gather sacred plants*
29 ● Cancer	30 WAXING	July 1 *Wear a silver charm* Leo	2 *Wish on the new Moon*	3 Virgo	4 *Trust to reason*	5 *Convene in a circle*
6 ◐ Libra	7 *Turn the world around*	8 Scorpio	9 *Let love find you*	10 *Accept a challenge* Sagittarius	11 *Don't disturb the spirits*	12 *Shop for worth* Capricorn
13 mead moon	14 WANING Aquarius	15 *Allow for error*	16 *Enjoy a chance encounter* Pisces	17 *Bright Mars glows*	18	19 *Laughter brings vitality* Aries
20 *Keep moving on*	21 ◑ Taurus	22	23 *Nomar Garciaparra born, 1973*			

THE HAZEL TREE

Coll — August 5 to September 1

Nine is a magic number, and the ninth consonant of the Druid's alphabet belongs to the tree of wisdom, poetic art, and divination—the magical hazel tree.

Unprepossessing to look at, more a spreading bush than a tree, the hazel rarely exceeds twelve feet in height. Bright brown bark mottled with gray, male and female catkins hanging like tassels, and oval leaves with toothed edges are identifying marks of the hazel. Hazel thickets provide winter cover for wildlife. Their branches in time past served as fences, pea poles, clothes props, and secured thatch for roofs of cottages. Excellent kindling wood, the hazel was the first choice of medieval bakers for their ovens.

The magical significance of hazel crosses many cultural lines, for it appears in the lore of Northern and Southern Europe and the Near East. The staff of the Roman god Mercury was of hazel wood. The myths say Apollo presented the caduceus to Hermes, the Greek counterpart of Mercury, in recognition of his mystical power to calm human passion and improve virtue. The medieval magician's wand was traditionally cut from the hazel tree with scrupulous ceremony drawn from Hebraic sources. Ancient Irish heralds carried white hazel wands. The "wishing rods" of Teutonic legend were cut from the hazel tree.

Hazel's function as a divining tool is many centuries old. The forked hazel-stick employed by dowsers to discover underground water sources, mineral deposits, and buried treasure is still in use today as it was before the turn of the Christian era.

Hazelnuts, often called filberts, are used as charms to promote fertility. Charles Godfrey Leland says "a rosary of hazelnuts brings good luck when hung in a house, and hazelnut necklaces found in prehistoric tombs were probably amulets as well as ornaments." Hazelnuts turn up in a variety of forms of love divination: share a double nut with someone you love and if silence is maintained while the nuts are eaten, your love will grow.

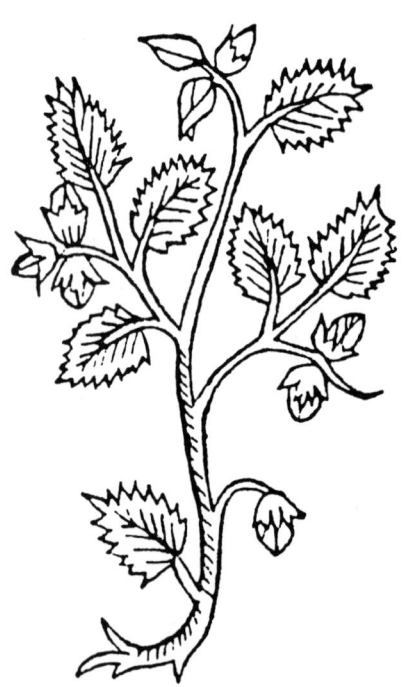

HAZEL
Corylus avellana

| ♌ | leo | July 24- August 23 |  |

Sun *Fixed Sign of Fire*

s	m	t	w	t	f	s
				July **24** *Choose the right time* Gemini	**25**	**26** *Wear red for courage* Cancer
27 *Fight lethargy*	**28** Leo	**29**	**30** WAXING	**31** *J.K Rowling born, 1965* Lughnassad Eve Virgo	Aug. **1** LAMMAS	**2** *Collect sacred water* Libra
3	**4** *Practice sorcery* Scorpio	**5**	**6** *Make no judgement* Sagittarius	**7** *Work a candle spell*	**8** Capricorn	**9** *Devote time to loved-one*
10 *Find time for folly*	**11** *Honor the Moon* Aquarius	**12** wort moon	**13** DIANA'S DAY WANING Pisces	**14**	**15** *Charles G. Leland born, 1824* Aries	**16** *Time to reap and store*
17 *Wear an amulet for luck*	**18** Taurus	**19**	**20** *Harvest your crops* Gemini	**21** *Rise to the occasion*	**22** *Shelter a lost one*	**23** *Drift with the tide* Cancer

Death and the Maiden

The Latin phrase *memento mori*, "remember that you will die," was a popular subject in medieval times. The Dance of Death motif is displayed in many art forms from music to tombstones. The tradition appeared first in France — *danse macabre* — before spreading throughout Europe. The theme of Death and the Maiden inspired one of the most beautiful of Shubert's songs as well as his brilliant Quartet in D Minor.

The woodcut above is from German incunabula (books printed before 1501). A jolly death figure with violin has a serpent in his mouth and a tiny bear on his skull. He greets the reluctant maiden and invites her to join the dance.

♍ virgo — August 24–September 23

Mercury *Mutable Sign of Earth*

S	M	T	W	T	F	S
Aug. 24	25 *Sean Connery born, 1930* Leo	26	27 Virgo	28 WAXING	29 Day of Thoth Libra	30 *Erase an error*
31 *Observe the sky* Scorpio	Sept. 1	2 *Speak no evil*	3 Sagittarius	4 *Collect white stones*	5 Capricorn	6 *Dismiss doubt*
7 *Try before you trust* Aquarius	8 *Share a secret*	9 *Jane Ellen Harrison born, 1850* Pisces	10 barley moon	11 WANING Aries	12 *Take a new route*	13
14 *Toss a gift to the sea* Taurus	15 *Scry for an answer*	16 Gemini	17 *Hope invites good luck*	18	19 *Bide your time* Cancer	20 *Collect fallen feathers*
21 *Call the corners* Leo	22 *Rely on memory*	23 Autumnal Equinox Virgo	24	25	26	27

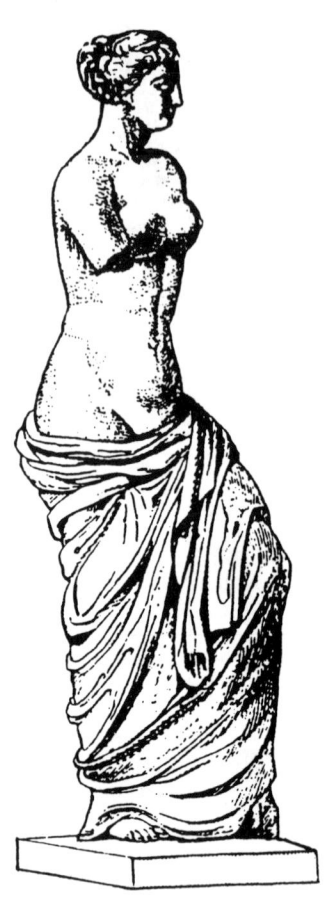

The Mystery of Venus de Milo

No one knows how the Venus de Milo, one of the world's most renowned statues, came to be buried on the tiny Greek island of Milos. No one knows who sculpted the marvel or what happened to the famous missing arms. The statue apparently had all her appendages when she was dug up in 1820 by George Kontrotas, a farmer. According to island tradition the left hand held an apple, the right hand held a belt. The belt legend is perplexing, since she is nude to her lower hips. An earlier statue by Praxiteles, the most sublime of the Greek sculptors, had been the first to depict the female nude. His masterpiece, a nude Aphrodite, shocked the populace, and most of the later depictions were at least half draped, as is the de Milo artist's version. She is ravishing, as befits the goddess of beauty, love and sexual rapture.

Today one of the glories of the Louvre, we have few facts but plenty of speculation about the statue. At her discovery the local French consul, struck by her splendor, made an offer to buy Venus for the Paris museum. Kontrotas agreed. But by the time the Comte de Marseilles arrived to negotiate the purchase, the farmer had sold it to the Turks. The French applied diplomatic clout, eventually gained possession, and Kontrotas was whipped for his double dealing. The farmer had unearthed the statue near the site of a very old gymnasium above a perfectly preserved Roman theater, giving rise to the theory that she may have been donated to the venue by a wealthy local merchant. The Greek name of the goddess is Aphrodite, yet the statue is always known as Venus, the Roman equivalent – logical enough had she graced a Roman structure. What we do know for sure is that fortune smiled on a Greek farmer the day he set out to work his land – and unearthed one of the magnificent art treasures of the ancient world.

libra
September 24 – October 23

Venus   *Cardinal Sign of Air*

s	m	t	w	t	f	s
			Sept. 24 *Divine the future*	25 ● Libra	26 WAXING	27 *Consult the I Ching*
28 *Stake a claim* Scorpio	29	30 *Integrity is essential* Sagittarius	Oct. 1 *Keep a promise*	2 ◐ Capricorn	3 *Eleonora Duse born, 1859*	4 Aquarius
5 *Maintain poise*	6 *Think on your feet* Pisces	7 *Clear the channels*	8 *Insist upon honesty*	9 Aries	10 blood moon	11 WANING Taurus
12 *Play a different tune*	13 *Be discreet today*	14 *Whistle up the wind* Gemini	15	16 *Habits are chains* Cancer	17 *Keep a low profile*	18 ◑
19 *Force fails* Leo	20 *Lessen stress*	21 *Music is the key* Virgo	22 *Franz Liszt born, 1811*	23 Libra		

Aubrey Beardsley, 1894

MASQUERADE

The November Eve sabbat is a night of illusion and fantasy. Strange notions of fear, beggary, mischief; guises of ghosts, goblins, and monsters have been imposed on a sacred and beautiful holiday. Clear your mind and return to the time when witchcraft had a life of its own; before the Church ruled, before the Renaissance, before the Age of Reason. November simply marks the prelude to winter's dark chill. The ancients sensed a need for courage, a ray of hope. Imagination can spark both.

"Dressing-up" is fun, still a child's favorite pastime, and appropriate to this sabbat. Have you dreamed of finding an old trunk full of wonderful costumes in a dusty attic? The extraordinary Lady Ottoline Morrell, hostess to the literary lights of England's Bloomsbury set, recognized this common fantasy. She would invite her guests to choose costumes from a chest filled with exotic garments: a mandarin's robe of heavy silk, a Turkish vest encrusted with jewels and gold ornament, the elaborate headdress of a Balinese dancer, masks, fans, and all manner of fripperies. Shyness was soon forgotten as artists, writers, statesmen and philosophers dressed up and enjoyed themselves enormously.

Witches are keenly aware of the psychological lift to the spirits a visual transformation can bring. A new persona enlivens what may appear to be a hopeless situation. Whimsy and a light heart are keys to joy. Witchcraft in America is the fruit of a tree transplanted from Europe centuries ago. Its truth is ancient and profound. November Eve celebrates the death of the year and welcomes the delights of a new cycle. Within the magic circle of death and renewal is the hidden challenge to change. Take a night off from rigid reality. Free your imagination. Whether you attend a fancy-dress ball, spend a quiet evening at home with family and friends, or perhaps alone in front of a mirror, perform a transformation just for the fun of it.

scorpio October 24-November 22

Pluto   Fixed Sign of Water

s	m	t	w	t	f	s
					Oct. **24** *A brown wind sighs*	**25** Scorpio
26 WAXING Gain an hour 2 a.m.	**27** Sagittarius	**28** *Turn the tide*	**29** *Gather resources* Capricorn	**30** *Demand the best*	**31** Samhain Eve Aquarius	Nov. **1** HALLOW-MAS
2 *Find the still point*	**3** *Reserve energy* Pisces	**4** *Touch an oak tree*	**5** *Peace returns* Aries	**6** *Enjoy the moment*	**7** *Health, wealth, friendship* Taurus	**8** snow moon Total lunar eclipse
9 WANING	**10** *Allow for change* Gemini	**11** *As above, so below*	**12** Cancer	**13** *Whoopi Goldberg born, 1949*	**14** *Clouds gather now*	**15** *Shun danger* Leo
16	**17** *Weave a magic spell* Virgo	**18** *Honor Theo tonight*	**19** *Trust your heart*	**20** Libra	**21** *Laughter will heal*	**22** *Hoagy Carmichael born, 1899* Scorpio

NEGATIVE CONFESSION

The Book of Coming Forth By Day is the name ancient Egyptians gave their mortuary texts, guides to the afterlife. These documents, collectively known to us as the Book of the Dead, form the Western world's oldest body of literature. A provocative section deals with the Negative Confession. Rather than lament and beg forgiveness, the deceased lists all the sins of which he is not guilty.

When you're feeling low and everything seems to go wrong, affirm your essential goodness with a Negative Confession. It's bound to lift your spirits and change your frame of mind.

> I have slain no man.
> I have caused no man to suffer.
> I have not domineered over slaves.
> I have not known worthless men.
> I have not committed evil in place of truth.
> I have not encroached upon the fields of others.
> I have not caused pain to the multitude.
> I have allowed no man to go hungry.
> I have not defrauded the poor man of his goods.
> I have not given the order for any man to be slain.
> I have not wronged my kinsfolk.
> I am pure. I am pure. I am pure. I am pure.

Translation by E. A. Wallis Budge.

sagittarius November 23-December 21

Jupiter   *Mutable Sign of Fire*

s	m	T	W	T	F	s
Nov. 23 ●	24 WAXING Sagittarius	25 *Achieve a goal*	26 Capricorn	27 *Bruce Lee born, 1940* Aquarius	28 *Seek more data*	29 *Compose a song*
30 ☽ Pisces	Dec. 1 *Inspire courage*	2 Aries	3 *Give credit when it is due*	4 *Bolster psychic energy*	5 *Christina Rossetti born, 1830* Taurus	6 *Work a fire spell*
7 *Honor the oak tree* Gemini	8 (oak moon)	9 WANING	10 *Eliminate negative thoughts* Cancer	11	12 *Love without bounds* Leo	13 *Reach for the stars*
14 *There is but one of you in all of time*	15 Virgo	16 ☾	17 Saturnalia Libra	18 *Be alert to danger*	19 *Challenge injustice* Scorpio	20 Eve of Yule
21 WINTER SOLSTICE Sagittarius						

A friend in need...

Of all things that wisdom provides to make life entirely happy, the greatest is the possession of friendship.
— EPICURUS

When a friend suffers a setback, illness or accident, magical gifts are in order. An ancient tradition calls for a quest, sacrifice or a blessing to turn bad luck into good luck.

THE QUEST

Effort is required to find this particular magical charm. Sites include the bed of a swiftly moving river or mountain stream, perhaps a beach where ocean tides churn pebbles to shore.

As the moon waxes to full set out to find a rock worn smooth to the shape and size of a plover's egg. Silently anoint the chosen stone with scented oil. Make a nest of sweet-smelling herbs to hold the charm, wrap in paper, and tuck away for safekeeping. Remove the stone from its hiding place at full moon and hold aloft in the wind to awaken its power and spirit. Present the charm to that person you wish well.

THE SACRIFICE

Sometimes a gift must be a sacrifice. Your choice may be one of your own treasured possessions, small enough to hold in your hand. Or browse through an antique shop until something catches your eye, an object you really want to own. Buy it without bargaining. Should you feel ambivalent later about giving it away, stay with your original purpose, for then the charm's power will be further enhanced.

Purify the gift in perfumed smoke to rid it of all previous influence. At Dark-of-the-Moon when all is still, hold the charm in cupped hands and gaze at it with all the force you possess. Imbue it with the power you feel coursing through your arms until the charm is completely charged. Place it then on a photograph of the one for whom the amulet is intended and mentally visualize all the goodness you wish the charm to bring forth. Let a series of images pass through your mind at their own pace until you can see no more. Wrap the gift in silk of an appropriate color (one that suits the recipient) and present it while the Moon is still a waxing crescent.

THE BLESSING

Oral tradition has successfully sustained the mystical thought of the Old Irish culture, in existence before the Egyptians built their pyramids. Recite the words aloud when the waxing Moon sets in the west to request good fortune for your friend.

> *Power of raven be thine,*
> *Power of eagle be thine,*
> *Power of storm be thine,*
> *Power of sun.*
> *Goodness of sea be thine,*
> *Goodness of earth be thine,*
> *Goodness of heaven.*
> *Each day be joyous to thee,*
> *No day be grievous to thee,*
> *Honor and compassion.*

♑ capricorn — December 22- January 20

Saturn Cardinal Sign of Earth

S	M	T	W	T	F	S
	Dec. 22 *The Wheel turns now*	23 ● Capricorn	24 WAXING	25 *Hum a happy tune* Aquarius	26	27 *Prepare for a miracle* Pisces
28 *Buy a bird feeder*	29	30 ◐ Aries	31 *Extend a helping hand*	Jan. 1 2004 Taurus	2 *Break the ice*	3 *Make a firm decision* Gemini
4 *Satisfy a craving*	5 *Sense a trend*	6 Cancer	7 wolf moon	8 WANING	9 *Day of Janus* Leo	10 *Consider the source*
11 Virgo	12 *Find a hidden potential*	13 *Avoid turmoil* Libra	14 *One step at a time*	15 ◐	16 *Solve a puzzle* Scorpio	17 *Ask no questions*
18 *Danny Kaye born, 1913* Sagittarius	19 *Tippi Hedren born, 1931*	20 *Well begun, half done* Capricorn				

Aesop's Fables — Ulm, 1476

The Wolf and the Crane

A WOLF once got a bone stuck in his throat. So he went to a Crane and begged her to put her long bill down his throat and pull the bone out. "I'll make it worth your while," he added. The Crane did as she was asked, and removed the bone quite easily. The Wolf thanked her kindly, and was just turning away, when she demanded, "What about my reward?" The Wolf, laughing and baring his teeth, said, "Now you can boast that you once put your head into a Wolf's mouth and didn't get it bitten off."

MORAL: When you deal with dangerous people, don't expect too much.

aquarius

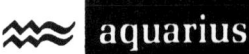 January 21-February 19

Uranus   *Fixed Sign of Air*

s	m	t	w	t	f	s
			Jan. 21 **Year of the Monkey**	22 WAXING Aquarius	23 *Lay a firm foundation*	24
25 *Cheer a lonely heart* Pisces	26	27 *Marat Safin born, 1980* Aries	28 *Assume command*	29 Taurus	30 *Trust an omen*	31 *Prepare for the sabbat*
Feb. 1 Oimelc Eve Gemini	2 CANDLE-MAS	3 *Collect sacred water* ☞	4 Cancer	5 *Discard doomed dreams*	6 storm moon Leo	7 WANING
8 *Lighten your burden* Virgo	9	10 *Elizabeth Barrett Browning born, 1806*	11 *Put your house in order* Libra	12 *Need not who needs not thee*	13 Scorpio	14 *Climb to the summit*
15 *Toss a token in a stream* Sagittarius	16 *Release tension*	17 Capricorn	18 *Collect your thoughts*	19 *Pause and observe* Aquarius		

35

Winds of the Rede

The winds are significant messengers of Nature, but only to those who listen carefully. The following verses can help you interpret the airy bulletins. The late Gwen Thompson, prominent in New England witch circles, drew these from her hereditary Book of Shadows, a rede derived from the witches of Somerset, England:

Heed the Northwind's mighty gale;
Lock the door and drop the sail.
When the wind comes from the South,
Love will kiss thee on the mouth.
When the wind blows from the East,
Expect the new and set the feast.
When the West wind blows o'er thee,
Departed spirits restless be.

The North Wind is powerful and must never be met head on; move into it shoulder first to show respect for its might. This wind brings transformation and must be greeted by willingness to recognize and bend with its power. The witch with the wisdom to understand the forces behind the great North Wind can harness such energy and transform it into a meaningful experience.

The South Wind brings the gentlest message, that of love. Its lesson is easily accepted, but sometimes difficult to understand. This wind predicts that we will soon be speaking of love and that the object of our desires will hear our gentle words. Take advantage of a strong South Wind to bring union, strengthen partnerships, make friends, and realize the gift we have been given throughout our incarnations.

The East Wind can be the most challenging, for "expect the new" keeps you wondering about what person or event is about to affect your life. Whatever it may be will cause change, and change usually brings stress or conflict before it brings stability. But this is the path to growth. The East Wind blows in a freshness to life and many new opportunities.

The West Wind is frequently misunderstood. The witch must realize that this can be a time to listen to the wind for messages from the dead. If you listen carefully, you will hear the voices of those you have lost, sending you words of love and remembrance.

— THEITIC

♓ pisces — February 20 - March 20

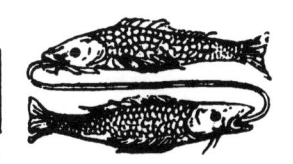

Neptune — *Mutable Sign of Water*

S	M	T	W	T	F	S
					Feb. 20 ●	21 WAXING Pisces
22 Frédéric Chopin born, 1810	23 Address the crescent Moon	24 Paula Zahn born, 1956 Aries	25	26 Weather the storm Taurus	27 ◐	28 Keep to yourself Gemini
29 Water assumes any shape	Mar. 1	2 Return a favor Cancer	3 Life is a banquet	4 Nature is never precise Leo	5 Honor purity	6 chaste moon
7 WANING Virgo	8 Reverse patterns	9	10 Scorn arrogant ignorance Libra	11 Welcome wild birds Scorpio	12 Remain within your limits	13 ◑ Sagittarius
14 The wind will guide	15 Capricorn	16 Court good luck	17 No time like the present Aquarius	18 Forget regret	19 An end is a beginning	20 ● Pisces

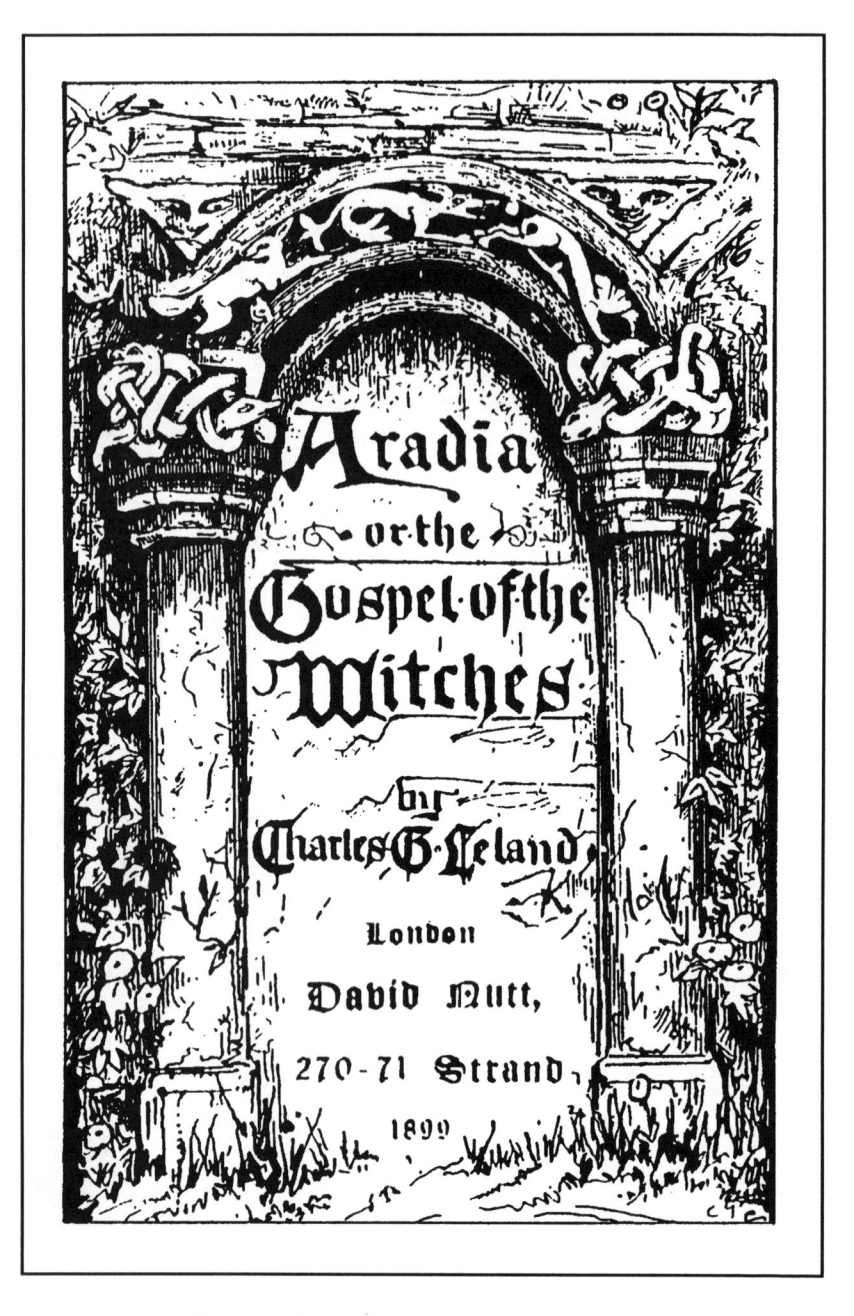

Title page from the first edition with art by the author. Leland illustrated many of his own books in distinctive style and with considerable skill.

Finding the Aradia papers

Just over a hundred years ago there appeared a literary harbinger of the modern interest in witchcraft as a religion. *Aradia, or the Gospel of the Witches*, was written by Charles Godfrey Leland, a Philadelphian who wrote and translated a variety of works about folklore, mysticism and the occult. To the casual reader the Aradia may appear to be a translation of secret scripture derived from *la Vecchia Religione*, the Old Religion of Italy. But the story of Aradia is more complex, for the book has its own hidden history and its own intriguing source clues.

I made efforts to follow these clues in libraries where Leland's papers had been preserved, hoping to find letters and manuscripts written by his foremost Italian informant, the woman he called Maddalena. Nothing from her hand emerged. But I did make an interesting finding among the fifteen boxes of Leland's papers at the Historical Society of Pennsylvania. I recognized a passage from the Aradia on a numbered sheet in Leland's handwriting. With mounting excitement I looked for other such pages among the jumbled contents of the boxes. When I finished searching and arranging, I had before me a discovery almost as good as Maddalena's missing manuscript. Here was Leland's complete handwritten text of the Aradia, which he had sent to the printer in 1899 and received back at the completion of typesetting.

With the assembled manuscript, I could see exactly how Leland had compiled the book from the variety of materials provided by Maddalena. On January 1, 1899, she had sent him *Il Vangelo delle Streghe*, the Italian version of the title. This was a short text and provided only the first two-and-a-half chapters of the Aradia. The remaining chapters obviously had been amassed by Leland from material he had secured from her over the years.

What do these discoveries mean for witches who still read the Aradia and Leland's other works on Italian magic and witchcraft? They remain valuable even though they present lore processed through the strong personalities of Leland and Maddalena. The *streghe* wove her own interests into the traditional material she collected for Leland, and he further shaped it according to his own personality. It is authentic folklore, for Maddalena was authentic, but it is untypical – for both Maddalena and Leland were notable for their eccentricities.

— ROBERT MATHIESEN

For more on *Aradia, or the Gospel of the Witches*, check out the latest edition, Phoenix Publishing, 1998, with contributions by Robert Mathiesen and other excellent scholars.

FAIRY GIFTS

IT OFTEN happens that people's surroundings reflect quite accurately their minds and dispositions, so perhaps that is why the Fairy Queen lived in a lovely palace with the most delightful garden you can imagine, full of flowers, and trees, and fountains. The Queen herself was so kind and good that everybody loved her, and all the young princes and princesses who formed her court were as happy as the day is long. They came to her when they were quite tiny and never left her until they were grown up and had to go away into the great world; and when that time came she gave to each whatever gift was asked of her. But it is chiefly of the Princess Sylvia that you are going to hear now.

The Fairy Queen loved her with all her heart, for she was at once original and gentle, and she had nearly reached the age at which the gift was bestowed. However, the Queen had a great wish to know how the other princesses who had grown up and left her, were prospering. Before the time came for Sylvia to depart, the Queen resolved to send her to some of them.

So one day the royal chariot, drawn by butterflies, was made ready, and the Queen said, "Sylvia, I am going to send you to the court of Iris; she will receive you with pleasure for my sake as well as for your own. In two months you may come back to me again, and I shall expect you to tell me what you think of her."

Sylvia was very unwilling to go away, but as the Queen wished it she said nothing — only when the two months were over she stepped joyfully into the butterfly chariot, and could not return quickly enough to the Fairy Queen, who, for her part, was equally delighted to see Sylvia again.

"Now, child," said she, "tell me what impressions you have received."

"You sent me, madam," answered Sylvia, "to the court of Iris, on whom you had bestowed the gift of beauty. Yet she never tells anyone that it was your gift, though she often speaks of your kindness. It seemed to me that her loveliness, which fairly dazzled me at first, had completely deprived her of the use of any of her other graces. In allowing herself to be seen, she appeared to think that she was doing all that could be required of her. But, sadly, while I was with her she became seriously ill, and though she presently recovered, her beauty is gone. She hates the sight of herself and is in despair. She entreated me to tell you what had happened, and to beg you to restore her beauty. And, indeed, she does need it terribly, for all the things in her that were tolerable, and even agreeable, when she was so pretty, seem quite different now that she is ugly. It has been so long since she considered using her mind or her natural cleverness, that I really don't think she has any left now. She is quite aware of all this herself, so you may imagine how miserable she is, and how earnestly she begs for your aid."

"You have told me what I wished to know," exclaimed the Queen, "but alas! I cannot help her; my gifts may be given but once."

Some time passed in all the usual delights of the Fairy Queen's palace, and then she sent for Sylvia again, and told her she was to visit the Princess Daphne. Accordingly the butterflies whisked her off, and set her down in quite a strange kingdom. But she had only been there briefly before she asked a wandering butterfly to take a message to the Fairy Queen, asking that she might be sent for as soon as possible, and before long she was allowed to return.

Illustrations by H.J. Ford

"Ah, madam," Sylvia cried, "what a place you sent me to that time!"

"What ever was the matter?" asked the Queen. "Daphne was one of the princesses who asked for the gift of eloquence, if I recall rightly."

"And very ill the gift of eloquence becomes Daphne," replied Sylvia, with an air of conviction. "It is true that she speaks well, and her expressions are well chosen; but she never leaves off talking, and though at first one may be impressed, one ends up being bored to tears. Above all things she loves any assembly for settling the affairs of her kingdom, for on those occasions she can talk and talk without fear of interruption. But even then, the moment it is over she is ready to begin speaking again about anything or nothing. Oh! how glad I was to come away."

The Queen smiled at Sylvia's distaste for her last experience, but after allowing her a little time to recover she sent her to the court of the Princess Cynthia for three months. At the end of that visit Sylvia returned to the Queen with all the joy and contentment that one feels at being once more beside a dear friend. The Fairy Queen, as usual, was anxious to hear Sylvia's opinion of Cynthia, who had always been amiable, and to whom she had given the gift of pleasing.

"I thought at first," said Sylvia, "that she must be the happiest princess in the world. She has a thousand subjects who vie with one another for her favors. Indeed, I had nearly decided that I would ask for a similar gift."

"Have you changed your mind, then?" interrupted the Queen.

"Yes, madam," Sylvia replied, "and I will tell you why. The longer I stayed the more I saw that Cynthia was not really happy at all. In her desire to please everyone she ceased to be sincere. Even those who truly loved her felt that the charm exercised upon all who approached without distinction was valueless, so that in the end they ceased to respond and went away disdainfully."

"I am pleased with you, child," said the Queen. "Enjoy yourself here for a while and presently you shall go to visit Phyllida."

Sylvia was grateful for the leisure to think, for she could not decide what gift she should ask for herself, and the time was drawing near. It wasn't long before the Queen sent her to the court of Phyllida, and waited for her return and report with keen interest.

"I reached her court safely," said Sylvia, "and she received me with much kindness, and immediately began to exercise that brilliant wit which you had bestowed upon her. I confess that I was charmed by it, and for a week thought that nothing could be more desirable. The time passed like magic, so great was the delight of her company. But I ended by coveting that gift less than any of the others. I realized that like the gift of pleasing, cleverness cannot give true satisfaction. By degrees I wearied of what had so delighted me at first, especially as I perceived more and more plainly that it is impossible to be constantly bright and amusing without being frequently ill-natured, and too apt to turn all things, even the most serious, into mere opportunities for a brilliant jest."

The Queen in her heart agreed. But now the time had come for Sylvia to receive her gift, and all the court assembled. The Queen stood in the midst of all and in the usual manner asked what Sylvia would take with her into the great world.

Sylvia paused for a moment, and then answered: "A quiet spirit." And the Fairy Queen granted her request.

This lovely gift makes life a constant happiness to its possessor, and to all who know her. She has all the beauty and gentleness and contentment in her sweet face. And if at times her looks seem less lovely through some chance grief or disquietude, the sharpest words one ever hears said are:

"Sylvia's dear face is pale today. It grieves one to see her so."

And when, on the contrary, she is joyful, the sunshine of her presence rejoices all who have the happiness of being near her.

— COMTE DE CAYLUS

The Count de Caylus lived during the reign of Louis XV, achieving distinction as a soldier, archaeologist and man of letters. He was a sophisticated member of Parisian high society, and this gentle tale contrasts with his reputation for sharp wit and a capricious nature.

What is your PSI potential?

Experts estimate that one person out of twenty possesses an unusual degree of extrasensory perception — ESP or PSI energy. University investigators of the paranormal have learned to expect certain characteristics from the successful candidates chosen to participate in PSI measuring experiments. The following questions may determine your own PSI potential:

1. Is it unusual for you to be reduced to tears?

2. Are you surprised to find yourself an object of conversation?

3. Have you ever said, "It just feels right" when reaching a positive conclusion?

4. Are you able to successfully visualize a room you knew as a child?

5. When speaking to an animal, do you use the same tone of voice and manner that you would in addressing another person?

6. Do you welcome adventure and enjoy solving a puzzle?

7. Have you ever sensed someone's thoughts while their words denied them?

8. Are you cheerful and optimistic by nature?

9. Does the atmosphere of a place influence your judgement of it?

Count your affirmative answers. Seven to nine mean your intuition is keen and should be developed. Four to six indicate your sixth sense is alive but needs trust and encouragement. Less than four makes us wonder why you're reading this in the first place.

presage

by Dikki-Jo Mullen

ARIES 2003 — PISCES 2004

There is a marvelous old tale recounted from a unique perspective each spring. Planets circle the Sun, while the Moon orbits the Earth. The circuit ends only to begin afresh. This perpetual celestial journey around the zodiac is the same, yet not the same. Each March when we note the first day of spring, as the Earth leaves the final degree of Pisces to cross to the first degree of Aries, humanity and the universe as a whole are a little older, a little more experienced than before. Astrology is a precious, ancient tool for the study of the journey. It steers us through the complex shimmer of cosmic energies which weave through our minds, hearts, and interactions with the greater world around us. Astrology guides us toward the discovery of all that's best of bright and dark.

June 3 finds serious Saturn changing signs to begin a three-year sojourn through Cancer. Respecting tradition, security, home, and family life will become a focus. The water supply and care of the very young and the very old can all be significant priorities.

On June 16, just before Midsummer Day, fierce Mars will begin an exceptionally long passage through mild Pisces. Mars usually remains from 6-8 weeks in a single sign. This time it spends half of the year in a single sign, not leaving Pisces until December 16. Much of the time it will be in retrograde motion. This does not favor triumph for aggressors. Subtle strategy is best. There can be a focus on the war against substance abuse. Those engaged in dream analysis, dance, or water sports will tend to progress while Mars is in Pisces.

Jovial Jupiter blesses Virgo by beginning a year-long transit there on August 27. This promises advancement in healing techniques, an overall interest in a wholesome diet, as well as appreciation for small animal companions. House plants and kitchen gardens will provide new delight and comfort to many.

The eclipse patterns in May and November will bring changing economic conditions and new ideas related to education, travel, and communication.

Read all about how these and other important heavenly portents will impact you and those closest to you in Presage.

ASTROLOGICAL KEYS

Signs of the Zodiac
Channels of Expression

ARIES: pioneer, leader, competitor
TAURUS: earthy, stable, practical
GEMINI: dual, lively, versatile
CANCER: protective, traditional
LEO: dramatic, flamboyant, warm
VIRGO: conscientious, analytical
LIBRA: refined, fair, sociable
SCORPIO: intense, secretive, ambitious
SAGITTARIUS: friendly, expansive
CAPRICORN: cautious, materialistic
AQUARIUS: inquisitive, unpredictable
PISCES: responsive, dependent, fanciful

Elements

FIRE: Aries, Leo, Sagittarius
EARTH: Taurus, Virgo, Capricorn
AIR: Gemini, Libra, Aquarius
WATER: Cancer, Scorpio, Pisces

Qualities

CARDINAL	FIXED	MUTABLE
Aries	Taurus	Gemini
Cancer	Leo	Virgo
Libra	Scorpio	Sagittarius
Capricorn	Aquarius	Pisces

CARDINAL signs mark the beginning of each new season — active.

FIXED signs represent the season at its height — steadfast.

MUTABLE signs herald a change of season — variable.

Celestial Bodies
Generating Energy of the Cosmos

Sun: birth sign, ego, identity
Moon: emotions, memories, personality
Mercury: communication, intellect, skills
Venus: love, pleasures, the fine arts
Mars: energy, challenges, sports
Jupiter: expansion, religion, happiness
Saturn: responsibility, maturity, realities
Uranus: originality, science, progress
Neptune: dreams, illusions, inspiration
Pluto: rebirth, renewal, resources

Glossary of Aspects

Conjunction: two planets within the same sign or less than 10 degrees apart, favorable or unfavorable according to the nature of the planets.

Sextile: a pleasant, harmonious aspect occurring when two planets are two signs or 60 degrees apart.

Square: a major negative effect resulting when planets are three signs from one another or 90 degrees apart.

Trine: planets four signs or 120 degrees apart, forming a positive and favorable influence.

Quincunx: a mildly negative aspect produced when planets are five signs or 150 degrees apart.

Opposition: a six sign or 180 degrees separation of planets generating positive or negative forces depending on the planets involved.

The Houses — *Twelve Areas of Life*

1st house: appearance, image, identity
2nd house: money, possessions, tools
3rd house: communications, siblings
4th house: family, domesticity, security
5th house: romance, creativity, children
6th house: daily routine, service, health
7th house: marriage, partnerships, union
8th house: passion, death, rebirth, soul
9th house: travel, philosophy, education
10th house: fame, achievement, mastery
11th house: goals, friends, high hopes
12th house: sacrifice, solitude, privacy

ECLIPSES

Eclipses occur when the light emitted by one heavenly body is completely or partially blocked by another. The most important of these mysterious and intriguing celestial events involve the Sun, Moon, and Earth. Eclipses have long had a prominent place in astrology; they have been linked to major world events and to the births of great people. The scientific world recognizes that eclipses have a profound impact on living creatures.

The practice of witchcraft recognizes the power of the lunar cycle and makes use of the waxing or waning power tides in magical workings. Eclipses mark times of special significance, when extra energy patterns are accessible and a glimpse into other dimensions occurs. If your birthday is on or near an eclipse day, prepare for a year of new awakenings, turning points, endings, and beginnings. If an eclipse conjoins a planet in your birth chart, that planet will be especially active in the year to come. Eclipses which conjoin the Moon's north node are generally considered more favorable than those conjunct the south node. Take note of the four eclipses in the year ahead.

May 15	Full Moon Lunar in Scorpio, south node — total
May 30	New Moon Solar in Gemini, north node — partial
November 8	Full Moon Lunar in Taurus, north node — total
November 23	New Moon Solar in Sagittarius, south node — total

PLANETS IN RETROGRADE MOTION

Retrograde motion actually means going backwards. Of course, the planets don't really switch into reverse, the effect is an illusion linked to the relative orbital speed of the Earth as compared to the retrograde planet. Retrograde motion is definitely felt in our lives, however, giving us a chance to regroup and reconsider.

Retrograde Mercury is the most common. Avoid travel to unfamiliar destinations, use care in signing contracts, expect visitors from the past. It usually lasts about three weeks, three or four times each year, and especially affects Gemini and Virgo people, who are ruled by Mercury. Here are the upcoming Mercury retrograde cycles:

April 26 - May 19
in Taurus

August 28 - September 20
in Virgo

December 17 - January 6, 2004
in Sagittarius and Capricorn

Mars retrograde does not favor the aggressor in war or other conflicts. There can be some tensions in the world of sports as well as in Martian pursuits such as engineering, heavy industry and construction. It's a good time to mediate and cultivate tolerance. The wise ones will get plenty of rest and take time for contemplation. Humor and patience are the best watch words under this pattern.

Mars will be retrograde in Pisces from July 29 - September 27, 2003.

All retrogrades give us opportunities to grow and learn through patience and repetition. As you study your own birth sign forecast in Presage, retrogrades involving other planets might be mentioned. Consider alternative ways to approach the situations suggested by the individual planets at these special times.

ARIES

The year ahead for those born under the sign of the Ram
March 21–April 20

You are characterized by natural leadership ability coupled with dreams of greatness. The first of the fire signs, the Ram cherishes goals which reflect inspiration, illumination, and idealism. Your strong sense of self can make you appear overbearing and argumentative, but this is a misinterpretation. You always retain a youthful exuberance and merely tend to be outgoing. By nature you make a conscious effort to express your individuality.

The vernal equinox finds Mercury entering your sign where it will move rapidly forward through April 5. Your thoughts are original and creative, so make notes. At the Aries New Moon on All Fools' Day, you will communicate with exceptional eloquence. During early April, Jupiter in Leo turns direct in your 5th house where it will remain until the end of August, making a wonderful trine to your Sun. The stars favor adding to your family. Creative projects will flourish as well.

On April 21 Venus enters Aries, and one of the most joyful cycles for romance and pleasure commences. By Beltane your charm and desirability opens important doors. Experiment with creative expression through mid-May. A grouping of Taurus transits in your 2nd house from May 15–June 11 accents security issues. Spend wisely and seek extra income opportunities. The May 15 eclipse can bring an interest in the afterlife, and perhaps a memory of another incarnation or a visit from an apparition. The May 30 eclipse in your 3rd house makes a neighbor or sibling anxious to communicate. During the first half of June Mars completes a passage through your 11th house. Try to avoid taking sides if friends are squabbling.

As Midsummer Eve approaches the Sun joins Saturn in your home and family sector. Relatives need extra love and care, especially if they are being difficult. You will long to repair, redecorate, or exchange your dwelling. Focus on spells and rituals to bless the home at the solstice. Remedy troublesome domestic situations before July 29 when Mars in Pisces begins a two-month-long retrograde cycle in your 12th house. By Lammas you will feel this planetary influence. You will be uncharacteristically reserved. Dreams and solitary reverie will help in problem solving. This cycle, which ends on September 27, is perfect for communing with nature. Consider primitive trekking or camping expeditions to heal and balance your psyche.

September begins with Jupiter, the Sun, Mercury, and Venus all in Virgo in your 6th house. Experiment with a new health regimen. Resist the urge to be impatient or finicky. On October 10 the Full Moon in your sign awakens you to new possibilities and your sense of humor returns. A mystery is solved the week before All Hallows Eve when Mercury joins Venus and the Sun in your 8th house. A friend or relative has some innovative ideas about finances and investments to share November 1–12. The eclipse November 8 accents changing financial situations. Flexibility is essential.

Your career prospects will be most promising from Thanksgiving through Yule. Venus will be in your sector of fame and fortune then. A friend can provide a professional opportunity. Don't hesitate to socialize with coworkers during the winter holiday season. Early December would be an ideal time to offer presentations to groups. When Mercury is retrograde from December 17–January 6, don't change jobs or try new ideas at work. Ignore office gossip at a holiday gathering.

New Year's Eve of 2004 finds your energy level high. Mars will be in the early degrees of Aries then, moving toward a trine with Pluto in your brother fire sign of Sagittarius. The momentum of this transit will open new levels of success and personal awareness through Candlemas. A yoga or martial arts program could be very rewarding. Since the 9th house is involved it's also the perfect time to enroll in a challenging academic program or to travel to sacred sites for spiritual nourishment.

The first week of February can find you juggling career responsibilities and family life, for Mercury and Saturn are in an opposition aspect impacting those areas. Reflect upon priorities; by February 7 the tension lessens. Finances should brighten when Venus is in your birth sign February 9–March 5. Curb impulsive spending then, for a Saturn influence in force at the same time could tempt you to run up credit cards. Treat any unwanted admirers with sensitivity and kindness. Good manners are a must near Valentine's Day.

Mercury's entry into Aries on March 13 through winter's end brings heightened intuition. The cosmic messenger will make a favorable aspect to Neptune, the ruling planet of psyches, perception, and dreams. If you have always wanted to learn to read the Tarot, meditate, or interpret dreams late winter is the time to do so. You will progress quickly with such studies.

HEALTH

Jupiter, the heavenly healer, will enter your wellness sector on August 27, conjoining the New Moon. This is a powerful combination of cosmic energy. It combines with a retrograde Mercury in the same house in your birth chart. This provides an excellent chance to overcome existing health challenges or to eliminate any bad health habits. The potentials for healing generated by this pattern will linger throughout the rest of the year. Mars will make a very long passage through your 12th house from mid-June until just before Yule. Be aware of how your mental attitude is affecting health then. Strive to battle depression by exercising. Remember to give thanks to the Lord and Lady for your many blessings.

LOVE

Spring and early summer will be most promising for love. Jupiter will be in Leo, sign of the heart, in your 5th house of romance then. An existing relationship will develop new depth; love experiences will be especially nurturing. Your beauty and charisma will peak from April 22–May 18 or from February 9–March 6, when Venus is in your birth sign. You tend to be very trusting upon first meeting an attractive prospect. Remember to take enough time to get acquainted before allowing yourself to think you've fallen in love. It might just be an infatuation.

SPIRITUALITY

Old journals, letters, and photos can serve as sources of spiritual awakening and rejuvenation near May 30 when an eclipse in your 3rd house aspects Neptune. Discuss metaphysical books in late November when another solar eclipse impacts your 9th house. This could also provide a valuable catalyst for heightening your awareness. Keeping a personal journal of perceptions and memories can be most valuable this year. Start the diary on your birthday. Begin at once and do the best you can. By Candlemas you will be amazed by how much you have accomplished. You might very well end up with a book worthy of publication by winter's end.

FINANCE

From June 3 through the end of the year Saturn will clamp down on your 4th house. Budget for a rent increase or home maintenance costs. A family member might require a loan following some unwise financial decisions. Consider offering advice and emotional support rather than letting another deplete your reserves. The lunar eclipses in May and November dynamically affect your finances. Explore new avenues of income and alternative career strategies. Your success this year may depend upon how well you are able to adapt to changing economic conditions in the world around you. Since you are by nature inclined to be a pioneer, this should be easy enough to accomplish.

TAURUS

The year ahead for those born under the sign of the Bull
April 21–May 21

With Venus as your ruling planet, loving and being loved is an important focus. A preference for beauty and comfort always leads you to insist upon quality. Your opinions are strongly ingrained and you'll resist change when it's forced upon you too strongly. The Bull has been a patient and reliable companion to humanity since earliest times. As your namesake suggests, you are loyal, affectionate, and usually predictable.

Uranus perches on the cusp of your 11th house as spring begins. Your social circle is interesting but especially changeable all year. You must prepare to say goodbye to old friends while greeting new ones. Your priorities are shifting. Take the time to do some soul searching from the vernal equinox until your birthday, defining what it is you really want. From April 5–June 12 Mercury will pass through your birth sign. This is a wonderful time to complete educational programs or travel to a reunion. A solution to a long standing problem can be developed while Mercury is retrograde from April 26–May 19. The lunar eclipse on May 15 accents new cycles in partnerships and relationships. Permit those closest to you to move forward and grow. This will enhance the love you share.

Late May through June 9 Venus will be in your birth sign. It will form a strong T-square aspect pattern with Jupiter in Leo as well as Mars and Neptune in Aquarius. You will enjoy living on the edge a bit. An adventure can end differently than expected, but at least life will be interesting. Keep a perspective on emotional involvements and how attachments impact your choices. Magical workings on Midsummer Day should focus on protecting the comfort and welfare of loved ones.

During the first half of July Mercury, Venus, and the Sun will join Saturn in your sector of transportation and communication. Shop for a vehicle, purchase travel tickets, and compose important letters. Conversations during this time can provide helpful ideas and perspectives. At Lammas friends need support. Both Mars and Uranus are retrograde in the sector of friendship and group involvements throughout August. Overcome impatience and try to help. With benevolent Jupiter and gracious Venus in your home and family sector during the first three weeks of August, real estate transactions and plans to renovate your dwelling may turn out to be a spectacular success.

September finds Mercury and Jupiter in your sister earth sign of Virgo brightening your 5th house of creativity and pleasure. Act upon creative ideas. Prepare a garden or collect autumn herbs and grasses to include in healing or prosperity rituals. Those desiring a child or interested in a romantic involvement can move closer to the realization of their dreams by the autumn equinox. During October your 6th house is highlighted by the Sun, Venus, and Mercury. You will be intrigued by coworkers and could develop closer friendships with them. Don't become too swept up in job politics, however. Your health can be improved by experimenting with color and sound therapies during the cool and crisp evenings of mid-October.

As All Hallows nears others will make plans for you. Cooperation is important. Expect good news involving a legal matter or other official business near October 26. The eclipse at the Full Moon of November 8 is in your sign. This is an optimum time to draw down the Moon with rituals dedicated to self improvement, health, and independence. New insight into who you really are comes into focus by the month's end. From November 16–30 a Mars-Jupiter opposition in the 11th and 5th houses shows that a friend could be jealous or troubled. You could be called to mediate a disagreement between companions. Annoying as this may be, your help will do much good.

The weeks before Yule should be especially joyful. Venus will make a wonderful trine aspect to your Sun while transiting Capricorn during the first three weeks of December. With Mercury supporting this cheerful planetary influence, holiday travel should be especially enjoyable. News from longtime friends and relatives will recall happy memories and honor traditions near New Year's Eve.

As 2004 begins Mercury and Pluto will impact your 8th house and make a quincunx aspect, suggesting some awkwardness involving a loan or investment. Companions have different financial priorities than you. The dilemma is resolved after January 15. Friends have joyful announcements and interesting plans to share as January ends for Venus will conjoin Uranus in the sector of friendships and future hopes. Just after Candlemas Mars will enter your sign and remain there through winter's end. Direct feelings of anger toward creating positive changes. You might feel drawn toward an exercise program. Winter will culminate with the world literally falling at your feet for Venus enters your birth sign on March 6 and will move into conjunction with Mars while in trine to Jupiter. This celestial pattern is especially favorable for improvement in both matters of the heart and of the pocketbook.

HEALTH

Treat yourself to a warm scarf, a pair of comfortable ear muffs, or a new hat to cushion your ears and neck against chills and wind. Experiment with ear candles to draw out wax and impurities from the ear canal, then listen to soothing music. Your birth sign points to the condition of the ears and sensitivity to sound having a powerful impact on overall health. The eclipses in May and November will bring your attention to any health situations requiring care.

LOVE

The most promising cycles for love this year are at the very beginning of the year, the period just after the vernal equinox, and again at the very end of the year, following the Candlemas holiday. Venus will transit your sign then. The eclipse pattern affects your partnership sector in a powerful fashion, signaling that a relationship could either end or begin. Don't resist change. With Jupiter moving into the 5th house of romance in earthy Virgo in the late summer, arranging a camping trip or planting a garden with an attractive companion could set the scene for an idyllic love interlude in September.

SPIRITUALITY

Your workplace will bring opportunities for a deeper spiritual realization. Mystical Neptune will influence your 10th house while making a high energy and challenging square aspect. Add crystals, statues of a favorite religious or mythological figure, or other charms to your desk. Affirmations as you travel from home to your job can be especially uplifting. Seek employment which nurtures the soul as well as providing material security.

FINANCE

A pattern of fixed sign planets in square aspects pivoting around Jupiter, planet of wealth, could point to potential financial frustrations early in the year. Resolve to overcome any counter-productive habits you may have and avoid acquiring debt through Lammas. When Jupiter enters Virgo on August 27 the situation should begin to improve significantly. Near the autumn equinox or at Yule holiday an easy and very effective money charm can be created.

Seek a small, attractive box, add a dried bay leaf, a handful of cedar wood shavings, and mingle in some favorite and treasured coins. Hold the box open under the sky during a waxing Moon and ask for abundance. Close the lid and keep it among your treasured possessions, tools of the craft, or sacred herbal plants. Occasionally shake the box.

GEMINI

*The year ahead for those
born under the sign of the Twins*
May 22–June 21

Your emblem, The Twins, shows that the stars have given you a great latitude of choice. In pulling the two sides of your mind together, you can create harmony and unity while rising above ambivalence and inconsistency. The need to make contact and to relate is integrated into all that you do. Communication and travel are especially linked to Mercury, your ruling planet. Focus on the classical image of the god Mercury. Swift, agile, and a mental step ahead of others, this archetype illustrates the brightest potentials within Gemini.

Spring brings a calm and reflective mood. You'll be aware of how much you've grown and how much stronger you've become. Saturn, the heavenly taskmaster, is completing a passage through your birth sign. The last couple of years have brought responsibilities and a few disappointments. You know now that you are about to overcome them and move forward. Contact friends and exchange ideas through April 4 while Mercury is in Aries. From April 5–June 12 Mercury will hide in your 12th house. Much of that time it will be in retrograde motion. Create a wholesome mind set and direct your imagination toward positive creative projects. You must make your own happiness now. Visualizations can generate powerful magic at Beltane. Revel in the freedom which comes from time spent alone.

April 22–June 16 Mars joins Neptune in Aquarius. Both planets will trine your Sun, the source of all life and energy. Physical activity usually bores you, but it will become enjoyable during this cycle. The 9th house is involved, so foreign travel or studies could appeal to you. The May 30 solar eclipse in your sign promises a memorable birthday. Be receptive to sudden opportunities. Flexibility and a progressive outlook will guide you toward success.

Just before Midsummer Day Mercury and Venus will enter your birth sign. From mid-June until the July 4 holiday you will receive invitations and can enjoy love opportunities. Life will be especially bright and beautiful during the week of the New Moon on June 29.

Competition and the realizations of ambitions will absorb you during July, for Mars in your 10th house will make strong aspects to other mutable sign transits, especially Pluto. There can be some professional politics to play. A stellium of planets in your 2nd house throughout July accents financial matters. You will want to boost earning power but must be patient with finances.

At Lammas Mercury crosses into your home and family sector. By the end of August it's joined there by benevolent Jupiter. If you are seeking different living arrangements August can bring some prospects. Communication with family members is improving. September commences with both Mercury and Mars retrograde in square aspect to your Sun. The force of habit can't be denied. A sense of déjà vu prevails. There is conflict between family life and professional aspirations. At the autumn equinox dedicate a ritual to release and recovery. The fall begins with Uranus retrograding back into Aquarius where it will form a trine with first Venus, then Mercury and the Sun in Libra, during the weeks before Halloween. This bright, airy combination should brighten your overall quality of life during October. Romance is especially promising near the Full Moon of October 10.

During the first half of November it's easy to be overly critical. Your 6th house is impacted by an awkward aspect pattern involving Mercury and the Aquarius transits. Seek ways to release stress. The eclipse of November 23 shifts your attention toward teamwork and partnership. December finds a career situation culminating, perhaps with a promotion or job change. The Full Moon in your sign on December 8 brings the specifics into view. Just before Yule Mars will change signs, leaving your 10th house for the first time since June. Suddenly pressures and anger will dissolve. There's a sense of peace about your profession and reputation. Circulate and accept invitations near the winter solstice.

New Year's Eve 2004 finds Mercury retrograding back into Sagittarius to join Pluto until January 14. Legal matters can require some attention–don't postpone this. Listen carefully to others, for a valuable idea can be suggested. Throughout the remainder of January through February 7 Venus adds ease and harmony to your workplace. Combine business with pleasure. A professional associate becomes a true friend near Candlemas. Rituals for success and recognition can be very effective during the first week of February. February 7–25 Mercury moves rapidly through Aquarius, sign of its exaltation, in a trine your Sun. This creates an optimum cycle for overseas travel, visiting your favorite libraries and book stores, or writing for publication. The pattern also favors the purchase of a new computer or automobile. Friends will be especially caring and affectionate from Valentine's Day through March 5 while Venus is in your 11th house. Enjoy companionship, but clarify your feelings if you aren't reciprocating a budding romantic mood. Throughout the remainder of the winter both Venus and Mars will be tucked away in the 12th house. You will cherish peace and privacy. Usually a chatterbox, you will find yourself being more discreet and reserved in mid-March. Pursue opportunities to do others a quiet kindness. Being a source of hidden support will uplift you in subtle yet powerful ways.

HEALTH

The May 30 solar eclipse in Gemini will bring new insights into wellness. Explore alternative remedies and changes in your fitness program. Write affirmations concerning strength and health late in the evening on the day of the eclipse. Review these during your daily meditations in the months ahead. Saturn, the special indicator of health and age, leaves your birth sign on June 3. After that your vitality will improve considerably. A chronic health problem can be overcome.

LOVE

Near Midsummer Day Venus will brighten your birth sign. Explore romantic prospects during June and early July. A collection of well aspected Libra planets in your 5th house of romance during late September through mid-October promises some fun and happiness as well. The eclipse of November 23 exactly conjoins your 7th house of marriage and partnership. This brings signs of a change in marital status as well as important plans and suggestions from others near Yuletide. By the end of the year new bonds will be established. Let go of a relationship you've outgrown.

SPIRITUALITY

Your dreams can provide spiritual inspiration, for Neptune lingers in your 9th house all year. Keep a dream journal and form a dream study and discussion circle with coven members this year. Astounding spiritual insights will develop. You would enjoy learning about other beliefs and perhaps borrowing from other religions when Uranus joins Neptune in the 9th between September 14–December 30. A friend might encourage you in pursuing a new spiritual practice then.

FINANCE

Saturn is beginning a transit through your 2nd house of finance in early June. Be patient and add to earnings slowly. A windfall isn't in the stars this year, but patient effort will be rewarded. The generosity of another could augment your own earnings. A square from Jupiter in Virgo after August 27 through the end of the winter will tempt you to take a risk or make a major purchase. Approach this with caution; it's better not to overextend.

CANCER

*The year ahead for those
born under the sign of the Crab*
June 22–July 23

Children of the Moon are characterized by responsiveness, sensitivity, and emotional expression. Like the Moon, you fluctuate. Water has a special ability to balance and bring out the best in you. A walk along the shore will shift a negative mood. The Crab is acquisitive. Clinging to keepsakes and memorabilia often turns into a worthwhile avocation. Coming to terms with the poignant memories of formative years and acceptance of parents, especially the mother figure, play an important part in finding happiness for those born under this sentimental sign.

Spring begins with an intense and profound mood. Pluto makes a station then turns retrograde in your 6th house. Animal companions can require some loving attention and perhaps a check-up with the vet. On a personal level, be aware of health habits. Resolve to overcome any factors which might undermine wellness early in the year. Mars is in opposition to your Sun while transiting Capricorn until April 21. Argumentative and demanding individuals may enter your circle. Cope with humor and calmness. Avoid initiating lawsuits or promoting competitive situations at this time. Others insist upon taking the initiative. Let them.

After All Fools' Day Jupiter turns direct in your money sector while Venus is trine your Sun. This combination is especially promising for finances during the 2nd and 3rd weeks of April. Pursue opportunities to add to your income or enhance salable job skills.

May Eve brings word from old friends as the Sun joins retrograde Mercury in your 11th house. Past life regressions can be especially vivid during May and could bring insights about future goals. Mars and Neptune transiting the 8th house together late in the spring promise deepening perceptions concerning the afterlife. This influence can also bring some tension linked to shared finances. Control your own purse strings during May and June. On June 3 Saturn begins a three-year passage through your sign. Thoughts turn toward security issues. Fulfilling your responsibilities leads to true happiness during the months ahead. At the summer solstice sabbat, focus on gaining a deeper understanding of yourself, including your limitations.

Mercury and Venus will dance through your sign near your birthday. Both will trine Mars and Uranus in Pisces, your sister water sign. Late June through July is a perfect time to vacation, especially if you're choosing a cruise. A romantic interlude with a well traveled and well educated individual can lead to a long term relationship. At Lammas explore ways to boost earnings. With both benefics, Venus and Jupiter, in your 2nd house of finance during the first three weeks of August, a pay raise is very likely. Moon children seeking employment should receive promising job offers.

September promises closer rapport with siblings, for Jupiter will join three other major transits in the 3rd house. Strive for clear communication. A neighbor can become more important. Resist the temptation to try juggling too many projects at once. After autumn equinox the tension subsides and it will be easier to focus. On October 9 Venus enters Scorpio and forms a grand trine in water signs with Mars in Pisces and Saturn in Cancer. This extremely favorable trend brings positive experiences your way through the rest of October. The workload is easier to handle, and there is time for love and relaxation. Try making craft items that echo the past to give as gifts. All Hallows should be particularly magical and full of sparkle.

November 1–11 a very positive Mercury influence will enable you to understand children well. Listen carefully to loved ones and a new rapport will develop. This is an optimum time for travel too. Network at the Full Moon eclipse November 8. Friendships can move to a deeper level. Others will offer you the emotional support you need. The last three weeks of November bring a beneficial Mars influence combined with favorable transits in the health sector. Ills of the mind and body can be healed. A new strength and confidence develops by Thanksgiving.

Allow others to make plans for Yule. Venus will oppose your Sun, showing some differences in taste and preferences. Adopt a live-and-let-live attitude. Mercury and Saturn are both retrograde as the year ends and will be in opposition. This encourages only short journeys and favors maintaining the status quo. Don't overdo it with winter sports. If memories flood your thoughts near New Year's Eve, make a conscious effort to focus on the happy recollections.

Begin work early as 2004 commences. Much is expected of you and rewards will come if you don't disappoint. The Full Moon in your sign on January 7 will illuminate the specifics. On January 15 tensions lessen, for Venus will enter Pisces creating harmony which will last until February 8. At Candlemas friendships will unfold in spiritual or academic environments. Artistic talents will blossom too. Throughout the rest of the winter a favorable Mars sextile involving the 11th house continues to bring support from friends. Involvement with organizations is rewarding during late February and March. A friend will boost your confidence with encouraging suggestions.

On March 8 Saturn will complete a retrograde in your birth sign. It will no longer be possible to postpone facing a responsibility. The winter ends with a serious mood prevailing. Make this constructive rather than somber.

HEALTH
Family health history can provide valuable clues about wellness this year. Saturn entering your birth sign brings a message about heritage and age. Folk remedies can be effective; keep health care products on hand. The eclipse in your health sector on November 23 marks a turning point in strength and vitality. Prepare for it by exercising and eating well early in the year.

LOVE
The passion planets, Mars and Venus, will be trine each other in water signs during most of July and October. Love prospects will be bright during those months. Your ability to empathize, the exchange of sentimental tokens, and other small kindnesses can set the stage for romance. The May 15 eclipse creates some fireworks in your 5th house of love. An exciting new prospect can be drawn toward you, while an old involvement fades near that date.

SPIRITUALITY
Uranus will begin a seven-year transit through your 9th house of higher consciousness and spiritual awakening this year. Innovative mystical concepts are about to profoundly impact you. Esoteric astrology would provide a wonderful catalyst. Learn about your Vedic, Chinese, or Native American zodiac signs. At the Dark of the Moon an outing to a remote location, away from city lights, to stargaze would heighten spiritual awareness.

FINANCE
Develop financial opportunities early in the year. Jupiter, planet of plenty, will transit your money sector through August 26. The heavens will provide bounty then. Your future security will be determined by how you cherish and nurture the gifts given. Saturn's entry into your sign in early June will bring hints about future financial needs and long-term economic conditions. The Crab is the birth sign of more millionaires than any other in the zodiac. Dedicated effort now could allow you to join their ranks in years to come. Saturn's retrograde from October 25–March 8 will bring a rare opportunity to right past mistakes regarding poor financial decisions.

LEO

*The year ahead for those
born under the sign of the Lion*
July 24–August 23

Dignified, warm, and flamboyant are descriptions linked to the Lion. A certain royalty of carriage and natural stage presence is pervasive. You tend to be highly visible. If traveling with a group, the others tend to step back and let you lead the way without even realizing they've done so. A creative outlet is important as well as recognition and appreciation.

Spring begins on a bright note, for the heavenly benefactor, Jupiter, is in your sign. Transits of the Sun, Mercury, and Pluto from the other two fire signs, Aries and Leo, surround you with light and promise. Situations with children are about to improve. Discussions about travel or spiritual subjects will provide a new outlook by April 20. On April 21 Mars enters Aquarius. A square with fixed sign transits, including the Taurus Sun forms. Through June 17 others will tend to challenge you. Be patient if there is a sudden lack of cooperation on the home front. The New Moon at Beltane impacts your 10th house of fame and fortune. Prepare a ritual dedicated to career issues. Moving your home or redecorating could be planned near May 15 when the lunar eclipse impacts your home and residence sector.

During June new goals come into focus as air sign transits favorably affect your 11th house. Saturn changes signs on June 3, starting a passage through the 12th house. You would prefer to be alone rather than with the wrong people. This trend points to some frustration regarding charity or service work. Be patient and make sure recipients do their part. June 1–13 can bring encounters with unsettling situations if traveling. Allow extra time for delays and don't neglect routine safety measures. Travel trends are more relaxed the last half of the month.

Just before Midsummer Day Mars begins a long passage through your 8th house. Thoughts will turn toward the afterlife and spirit world. A past life recollection may help you cope with current situations. This will be a background theme in your life until mid-December. You will have a special flair for probing beneath the surface. By Lammas Eve Venus will enter Leo. August will be a happy and productive time. Others exhibit care and concern about you.

During September, finances will be in the spotlight. Curious and chatty Mercury will join Jupiter and Venus in Virgo in your 2nd house, the money sector. There should be some worthwhile earning opportunities. Develop your salable skills to place yourself in greater demand. By the autumn equinox Uranus will retrograde into your 7th house. A relationship could begin or end suddenly. Partners are a source of surprise. Learn by observing human nature. October 6–24 a favorable Mercury sextile in your communication sector promotes clear conversation and decision-making. Make seasonal decorations and entertain at home on All Hallows for your 4th house is energized.

Don't struggle against changes involving your career near November 8, for an eclipse in your 10th house augurs a new cycle. Success depends upon your ability to make the best of shifting trends. The remainder of November accents love. Venus and Pluto coupled with an eclipse in Sagittarius will highlight your 5th house of romance. A startling awakening will indicate where true love really is available to you. November 23, date of the New Moon, can be significant.

Venus enters your health sector as December begins. Explore the healing qualities of art, music, and companionship.

Subtle energy fields will be evident in your health picture. Study diet and vitamin therapies as Yule nears. Mercury in Capricorn opposing Saturn in Cancer will impact the 6th and 12th houses in your birth chart. Both planets will be retrograde indicating that old patterns must be overcome to assure exemplary health in preparation for the New Year. Devote the winter solstice to healing magic. Place an aromatherapy bag scented with pine and sage on your altar, then carry it with you as a healing talisman in the cold days to come.

January finds Mars in Aries making a lovely trine to your Sun. Your vitality will improve. There is a new enthusiasm for travel and expansion. A study program or meditation circle can be a catalyst for new perspectives. At the same time unpredictable Uranus will move into a long-term transit through your 8th house. Use caution before forming financial partnerships. Loans you make may turn into gifts. Be wary of advice, and double check tax or insurance matters.

At Candlemas, relax and allow companions to set the pace and make the plans. The Full Moon on February 6 in Leo will reveal your full potentials to associates. Smile if you're the topic of a juicy story and just say, "All those tales being told about me? Well, they're all true."

By Valentine's Day Venus will be creating a happy pattern in fire signs. The stars are great for your social life and cultural pursuits through March 4. Saturn will complete its retrograde as winter ends, turning direct in your 12th house. Long-time blockages and phobias are clearing. A renewed sense of freedom and confidence builds as winter ends, and you'll work well alone. Wrap up in a cozy robe and burn the midnight oil on a work or creative project. The results are apt to be truly brilliant.

HEALTH
With Saturn, natural ruler of your health sector, moving into your 12th house, it's especially important to use care while in contact with those who are ill this year. Make enough time for regular health care and fitness programs. When Mars changes signs on December 16 your energy will improve. The Lion wears a rich and beautiful mane. Likewise, the Leo born are often blessed with thick, beautiful hair. Explore new coiffures or haircuts. By caring for your crowning glory your overall well-being acquires additional sparkle.

LOVE
Prepare for much excitement. An eclipse pattern in Sagittarius, your 5th house of romance, coupled with Pluto shows deep attraction and some meaningful romantic interludes. Mysterious, unpredictable, and talented individuals are about to enter your circle. Neptune impacting the 7th house promises an interesting liaison or two. Lammas is the sabbat to devote to working love magic. Venus will be in your sign during much of August, showing the potential for true happiness at a peak near your birthday.

SPIRITUALITY
Mars rules spirituality in your birth chart. Learn about sacred balefires and rituals involving candles and incense. These evoke a sacred mood which will be meaningful to you. Look into drumming and dancing too. Ceremonies which encourage spontaneous activity will be uplifting. Create a primitive, natural, or native atmosphere to facilitate a connection with the divine primal forces.

FINANCE
If you are cautious about acting upon risky advice from others, this should be a marvelous year for finances. A quincunx aspect from Mars and Uranus in Pisces in your 8th house could bring impractical business associates or partners your way. With Jupiter moving from your own sign directly into your money sector, your personal earning capacity appears wonderful. The November 8 eclipse in your 10th house points to major changes in your professional situation. Be progressive, realize that growth can come about if the old patterns are disrupted. It's not the time to be stubborn. Stay in tune with the latest trends in your field.

VIRGO

*The year ahead for those
born under the sign of the Virgin*
August 24–September 23

Virgo is deeply connected to the Earth herself, as is illustrated by the shaft of wheat cradled in the arms of the zodiacal Virgin. A well kept garden, beautifully natural yet orderly, is a wonderful, descriptive symbol for Virgo at her best. Your earthiness extends to a practical philosophical outlook and longing for financial stability. Dedicated attention to the details of any task you undertake earns you the admiration and loyalty of coworkers. Your symbol is not meant to suggest celibacy, but rather a self sufficiency and purity of spirit.

Virgos will welcome spring with vibrant feelings of passion and a creative spirit. Energetic Mars is moving through Capricorn, your sister earth sign and position of its exaltation, until April 21. Whether you choose to nurture a romantic bond, enjoy time spent with children, or devote yourself to an avocation, you will be busy. On April 5 Mercury, your ruler, will enter Taurus, another earth sign, for a long passage culminating on June 12. This is extremely favorable for writing, study, and travel. Relationships between grandparents and grandchildren will be rich and rewarding. A delayed goal or dream can finally be realized while Mercury is retrograde from April 26–May 19. On May Eve compose an affirmation relating to a second chance or starting over.

The May 30 eclipse dramatically impacts your working conditions. New job duties or even a new job might be coming your way. By Midsummer Day a competitive mood will develop because several mutable sign planets, including Pluto, will square and oppose you. Don't ask favors of others. Saturn will begin a long transit through your 11th house in June, where it will aspect your Sun by a sextile aspect. You might become more active within an organization or even enter politics. As summer commences you will be very serious about planning and setting goals.

Just before Lammas Mercury enters your sign, where it will remain until October 6. You'll process data and analyze facts with a flair that leaves others speechless. The role of teacher or advisor comes your way now. Jupiter enters Virgo for a year-long transit on August 27, day of the New Moon which is also in Virgo. This very positive pattern promises growth and an overall improvement in standard of living throughout the months to come. A sense of a new start will surround you near your birthday. Improvement in love connections can be part of this during the first half of September, for Venus will link with the other favorable Virgo transits then.

Your sector of possessions and security will be accented from September 16–October 24, so plan a shopping expedition. All Hallows finds some interesting calls and letters arriving. If asked to mediate a dispute, be sure to keep any personal bias concealed.

Spiritual awakenings and vivid dreams can occur at the lunar eclipse on November 8. It is well aspected in your 9th house. Throughout the rest of November there is a great deal of emphasis on your home and family sector, peaking near the time of the November 23 eclipse. Change is the keynote. Family members will want to progress and meet new challenges.

A joyful love cycle develops during the first three weeks of December. Venus will brighten your 5th house of pleasure. Winter sports, parties, and cultural events can all serve as the backdrop for experiencing a special relationship. The last days of December through January 6 Mercury will be retrograde in Sagittarius. This can make New Year's Eve hectic. Release stress through getting organized and trying a short meditation. From January 15 through Candlemas you will feel more stable and confident. A leisure time pursuit could become a career avenue during this time. Don't hesitate to combine business with pleasure. A new movie or theatrical production can make a strong impression.

Starting February 4 through the end of winter your health and energy will be superb. Mars will trine your Sun, generating a new strength and vitality. Exercise programs can be especially beneficial during late February. You'll be motivated and able to accomplish a great deal. The Full Moon on March 6 falls in your birth sign. It strongly aspects several planets in mutable signs. Information is revealed concerning the feelings and plans of another. You will become aware of what you are about to outgrow, both personally and professionally. That Full Moon also marks the start of a favorable Venus transit through Taurus. This will trine your Sun. A well educated or well traveled new friend can be a source of happiness. Mid-March is the perfect time to shop for fashions and jewelry. Finery chosen and acquired during the last days of winter will enhance your natural attractiveness.

HEALTH

Wellness is always a concern, for the birth sign of Virgo has long been linked to health. Mental attitude plays a pivotal role in how well you actually are physically. Focus on understanding health conditions and communicating with health care practitioners so you can alleviate anxiety about your body. Jupiter has a special link to healing. When it begins a year-long passage through Virgo at the end of August, expect improved health. Adopt a cuddly kitten or pretty parakeet. You are very attached to small animals. The love and pleasure an animal companion provides is often an effective medicine.

LOVE

Prepare for one of the most startling and interesting cycles you will ever experience regarding relationships. Mars and Uranus will both remain in your 7th house of marriage and partnership for many months. Old relationships can either assume new sparkle and excitement, or in some cases, end. Sudden new infatuations can transform your life. Venus and Jupiter, the pair of heavenly benefics, will join hands in your birth sign for the first half of September. Romantic happiness is very likely to come along then. Always be careful to compliment those whom you love and admire. You tend to show concern and affection by offering to solve problems for those you love.

SPIRITUALITY

Create an outdoor altar or meditation garden. Communing with nature will facilitate your spiritual growth, as will music. Remember that angels are usually portrayed with musical instruments. Singing or listening to a favorite song can open you up to the higher planes. The eclipse of November 8 falls in your 9th house of the higher mind. It also makes a strong aspect with Neptune, planet of the mystical. November promises to be a time of new spiritual revelations and directions. Try to meditate on the November Full Moon.

FINANCE

Prepare for some home repairs or family expenses. Your 4th house is quite prominent this year. The eclipse pattern also hints at new developments at work which might affect your earning ability. Flexibility and preparation are the keys to coming out ahead. If a new job falls your way, accept it as a gift from the universe and give it a try. This is especially likely to occur during May and June. Many of the old financial habits and rules are shifting. The late summer through the end of the year is more promising. In late August Jupiter will begin a year-long passage through your birth sign. This assures a cycle of greater wealth and an improved lifestyle.

LIBRA

*The year ahead for those
born under the sign of the Scales*
September 24–October 23

Your emblem, the Scales, is the only non-living emblem in the zodiac. True and perfect balance is seldom attained in our out-of-balance world, yet you strive to maintain just that. Resolving discord and achieving justice as well as beauty is important. The value of sharing and teamwork guide your approach to life always. Reform and justice are principles you will uphold.

An early spring romance buds with the beginning of the year. Venus, your ruler, is in your love and pleasure sector from the vernal equinox through March 27. Encourage the passion to flower by preparing a love philter or dedicating a rose-scented, coral candle to Aphrodite. During the first half of April Aries transits will oppose you, while Mars creates a tense aspect. Others can be preoccupied or just downright ornery. Ask no favors and avoid large crowds. The Full Moon on April 16 in Libra will make others notice and appreciate you anew. Your pleasant appearance and winning personality will open doors throughout the rest of the month. On April 22 Mars changes signs, moving into Aquarius, where it remains through the middle of June in a trine to your Sun. Your energy level increases, making it easier to exercise regularly and express creative ideas.

May Eve finds Taurus transits gathering in your 8th house. Your curiosity will be aroused, and you'll tend to probe. An old mystery can be solved as a result. Others will want to discuss finances with you. Neptune will turn retrograde on May 15 in your 5th house of love. This will remain in effect until October 23. The appearance of soul mate connections can be important. Sincerity can become an issue with a loved one. Keep ties on a spiritual and idealistic plane. Avoid anyone who exhibits addictive behavior. Keep your distance from the untruthful and untrustworthy.

Friday, June 13 marks the start of a favorable Mercury cycle which will last through the summer solstice. Pursue opportunities for travel. Letters and conversations can lead to really important learning experiences. Ambitions will stir during July as Saturn, accompanied by Venus and the Sun, will square your natal Sun. Your career will be especially important to you. Your flair for working with all types of people can lead to a worthwhile opportunity. Follow through in exploring offers which come your way now.

At Lammas both Venus and Jupiter will draw emphasis to your 11th house. Friends offer assistance. Any apparent problems can be easily solved if you will just confide in a comrade. Good will and companionship are extended to you throughout the first three weeks of August. As August ends, you will cherish a few stolen moments dedicated to peaceful reverie. Help comes your way from a hidden or unexpected benefactor. Don't question the boon, just enjoy your good fortune. When Mercury turns retrograde on August 28, a cycle begins when you must focus on being your own best friend. A careless word or deed could undermine promising potentials in your life otherwise.

The early days of September can find you rather anxious. Overcome vague fears by calling upon a favorite warrior god or goddess. On September 15 Venus enters your sign, and Uranus enters your brother air sign of Aquarius a few days later. This combination of cosmic influences is especially jubilant. You'll attract admiration and love. A new companion can change your life for the better. The autumn equinox through the New Moon in Libra on September 25 will mark the peak of this very upbeat trend. Experiment with creative expression and socialize.

Mercury will fly through Libra making favorable aspects to several planets, including Neptune, from October 6–23. Consider travel to a sacred site or visit an art gallery or boutique. It's also a perfect time to try creative writing. As All Hallows nears your focus will turn to finances. You will long to purchase some pricey items and will seek the means to pay for them at the end of October and early November. The eclipse on November 8 can bring financial assistance or ideas from another. There will be a great deal of commotion and many short outings during the rest of November because your 3rd house is strong. Remain focused, for the eclipse on November 23 can create distractions. Transportation issues may need attention.

December favors trying new holiday recipes, but count calories from December 1–21. Cardinal sign squares then could tempt you to overindulge. Mars enters Aries and moves toward an opposition with your Sun from just before New Year's Eve throughout January. Keep debates and rivalry good natured. Others can be quite assertive, but your winning charm and diplomacy can smooth over ruffled feathers and hurt feelings. Devote the Candlemas sabbat to rituals for peace and harmony. During February others have very different tastes and preferences. Celebrate diversity and smile. Tolerance will win you a valuable ally.

During the first week of March Saturn completes its retrograde in your career sector. Situations which have been developing in the background finally crystallize and you will have the opportunity to take on new projects. Impressions you make this month can affect your professional status for a long time to come. Work hard and do your very best during winter's last days. The effort will pay off.

HEALTH

Uranus will cross the cusp of your health house from March until early September. Expect some sudden changes in your health. Be aware of the role stress and other environmental factors play. It's always important for you to avoid conflict. As the celestial peacemaker you will tremble and weaken in the face of ill will. A tranquil atmosphere is the single best health factor you can seek this year. Because you have a natural love of the arts, a form of art therapy could enhance your wellness. Leaf through Carl Jung's work, then draw a personal mandala to describe your innermost concerns and your feeling about your health. Paint it in your aura colors.

LOVE

Seek a spiritual type of commitment this year, for Neptune is midway through a long transit in your love sector. Try discussing dreams or past lives with one whom you admire. Be philosophical and respect another's need for independence from September through December. A Uranus influence can alter the status quo regarding love. Whatever happens then really will be for the best eventually.

SPIRITUALITY

Until June 3 pragmatic Saturn will impact your 9th house of the higher mind. Seek practical help for real life issues through meditations and ritual work early in the year. From Midsummer Eve on, look for meaningful ways to combine a variety of different spiritual traditions. Visiting different worship services and ceremonies can provide a wonderful spiritual awakening. Talking and reading about spiritual topics can be very uplifting as well.

FINANCE

The May 15 eclipse creates a cycle of surprise impacting your money sector. Consider developing new salable job skills. Finances are volatile this year. Develop an awareness of shifting economic conditions in the world around you. This will be a key to achieving greater security. You prefer understated elegance and don't want to appear wealthy. However, your natural good taste and appreciation for life's luxuries can make your overhead high. Patience is an important step in developing your long-range financial plan now.

SCORPIO

*The year ahead for those
born under the sign of the Scorpion*
October 24–November 22

Your fighting spirit and great determination always help you to rally when the game of life gets a bit rough. Dwelling on revenge or allowing bitterness to linger will cloud your tremendous potential to transform the world around you for the better. The Scorpion, your symbol, suggests subtlety. Your true purpose and aspirations are marked by controversy and mystery.

The springtime finds you running an abundance of errands with Mars active in your 3rd house from the equinox through April 21. Efficient scheduling assures maximum accomplishment. On March 27 Venus enters your love sector to remain there through the first three weeks of April. Intimate relationships will grow more tender during the early days of spring. Share music and dance with one whom you would woo.

By May Eve several planets in fixed signs will aspect Jupiter in your 10th house. Your professional sphere is widening. There is opportunity, but many demands are placed on you. It's easy to feel overwhelmed. You might have to choose between business and a relationship. The eclipse in your own sign on May 15, under the Full Moon, will clarify which choice is best. That lunation marks the start of a significant period of self discovery. At the beginning of June Saturn will enter your sister water sign of Cancer and will trine Uranus in early Pisces, the other water sign. The support of these two weighty planets will be very beneficial to you. By Midsummer Eve you will be engaged in several exciting and worthwhile projects. Spiritual and academic pursuits are especially favored. At the same time June 1-12 finds Mercury and Venus opposing you. Seek compromise if others are a little complex and argumentative.

By Fourth of July companions will be loving and cooperative again, for Venus will begin a harmonious transit through Cancer. Your 9th house is exceptionally well aspected through July 28. Enjoy some foreign cuisine and music or plan a vacation abroad. At Lammastide Mars and Pluto, which co-rule your birth sign, are both retrograde. Throughout August be aware of which habits and patterns are beneficial and which are not. The interplay between your career and love liaisons can be a factor. Avoid challenging others, for an aggressive tactic on your part right now can backfire. On August 28 Pluto turns direct and you can release the past. A more progressive mood builds as autumn approaches. September finds four important transits in Virgo–Jupiter, the Sun, Venus and Mercury–sextile your Sun. All of this activates your 11th house. It's time to network. Politics or work within a service organization can be worthwhile. Friends inspire you to develop worthwhile goals.

At the autumnal equinox Uranus and Neptune in your home and family sector can bring some confusion to the domestic scene. A relative or extended family member is ready to make some changes. Look at different options. Assemble magical workings to bless home and hearth. The situation will improve by your birthday. During October Mars will be direct and Venus enters Scorpio. This promises a renewal of enthusiasm and creative energy.

The dual eclipse pattern in November brings a turning point in a partnership or commitment. Your financial sector is highlighted by the November 23 eclipse as well as simultaneous transits from Pluto, Venus, and Mercury. Your attitude toward security is shifting. Explore new ways to earn your own money. Early December is a time to listen carefully. A casual remark or short, informal note can contain valuable information. Your 3rd house of communication has good Venus and Mercury aspects.

Accept an invitation to take a short journey before December 15. By Yule Mars will enter your health sector, remaining there throughout January. Focus on wellness during winter's darkest days. Stay warm enough and don't let inactivity or stress undermine your fitness. At the winter solstice light a blessed candle dedicated to health. This Mars trend can make you a little critical of a coworker too. Work on tolerance and releasing stress.

In January Venus will bring joy to family situations. On January 7 Mercury will turn direct in your financial sector. A decision about money matters will be made shortly after that. Candlemas finds favorable water sign transits in Pisces and Cancer surrounding you. Your natural sensitivity will be heightened in a positive way. A love relationship improves and you can plan a memorable journey by the end of February.

Winter's end finds Mars prominent, opposing your Sun from the very strong willed sign of Taurus. Others have definite plans and suggestions. Try to be cooperative. Patience on your part can avert a confrontation. Teamwork holds the key to success during March.

HEALTH

Mars, which has a special link to health in your case, will be retrograde from late July through the autumn equinox. Since this will occur in Pisces, therapies linked to the water can have a wonderful impact on you. Try flushing out your system by drinking plenty of fresh spring water. A bath in Epsom or mineral salts or immersion in a whirlpool can be relaxing and rejuvenating. Stroll along a favorite beach and connect with water elementals. Try your expertise at seafood cookery.

LOVE

This year will be one of the most exciting and interesting in regard to romance that you have ever known. Uranus, the planet of sparkles and surprises, will make a rare sign change and enter your love sector where it will remain for most of the year. A friend can introduce you to your soul mate. Astrology and other metaphysical studies can enhance your understanding of love. Don't worry if an old relationship ends abruptly, especially near Beltane. Something better will definitely be waiting in the wings!

SPIRITUALITY

Your spiritual growth will assume new depth and meaning after June 3 when Saturn enters your 9th house of philosophy and higher thought. You will become more dedicated to regular meditation and ritual observances of the yearly high holidays. This will bring a new and stronger spiritual support your way. A coven leader, perhaps a high priest, of a different generation (younger or older) can be a source of great spiritual inspiration. You will become much more informed regarding spiritual practices and formal observances.

FINANCE

Over the past year your overhead has been quite high. Jupiter, ruler of your money house, has been in Leo creating a reckless aspect to your Sun. At the end of August this transit ends and Jupiter moves into earthy Virgo. Your coffers will begin to be replenished. November brings some surprise offers and earning opportunities, for an eclipse impacts your finances. Be receptive to the idea of developing a new job skill or accepting a transfer. Changing to accomodate shifting economic demands in the world around you is very important if you are to be really successful.

SAGITTARIUS

*The year ahead for those
born under the sign of the Archer*
November 23–December 21

Elevating yourself and those you care about is at the heart of your mission in this life. The Archer aiming skyward at a distant target shows how you seek to transcend. His drawn bow illustrates unrealized potential seeking a worthwhile point of release. Devotion to a meaningful cause is important. Sagittarians make life an ongoing adventure in learning and experiencing. Yours is the closest of all the birth signs to really connecting with the world of animals.

As spring stirs Mercury will slip into Aries, creating a beautiful fire sign trine, along with the Sun, in your love and pleasure sector. This will peak at the New Moon on All Fools' Day and extend until April 5. Plan a jaunt with a loved one, maybe for a picnic in the forest or an evening drive to see a play in another town. A conversation inspires you creatively at this time. You'll work hard to acquire greater financial stability during most of April, for Mars is in your money sector.

At Beltane Venus and Jupiter, the great celestial benefics, both transit fire signs aspecting you well. You are loved and popular. You will find study satisfying throughout May. During June you will become absorbed in some research work, for your 8th house is accented. The pieces of the puzzle fall into place by the time of the Full Moon in Sagittarius on June 14. The lunation is tinged by Pluto and can trigger some past life recollections and an urge to follow through with self-improvement programs. Midsummer Day brings Mars into a long transit through your home and family sector. This will be in force until your birthday. Living arrangements are a source of tension.

July 13-29 finds Mercury joining Jupiter in your brother fire sign of Leo. Books and magazines can provide valuable perspectives. Foreign films or travel, perhaps to Latin America, would be rewarding and enjoyable. By Lammas Eve a mutable T-square aspect will affect the angles in your birth chart. August will be hectic but interesting. Double check directions, appointments, and information for accuracy. The end of the month finds ruling Jupiter changing signs. Your career is about to enter a whole new phase. Be receptive to growth. You're due for added recognition in the weeks ahead.

September finds retrograde Mercury also affecting your career sector. Tie up loose ends. Prepare for new horizons to open near the autumn equinox when the retrograde is complete. Friends are very concerned and kind to you as September ends for Venus will be well aspected in your 11th house. An artistic or well mannered companion adds a note of genuine culture and harmony to your life from September 15–October 9. The days preceding Samhain find the lone wolf part of your nature surfacing. Spend part of the holiday in solitude. A dream or deep meditation can provide meaningful guidance.

November is most promising in regard to romance. On the 2nd Venus enters your sign and you no longer yearn for privacy. By the 11th Mercury is also in your sign. The eclipse pattern in November can be significant regarding health care. Be sensitive to what your body tells you and all will be well. Being a fire sign, you revel in excitement. November brings you plenty of that with a total eclipse of the Sun in your sign on the 23rd. Changes starting now will unfold for many months to come. Enjoy.

Finances need attention during the first half of December when Capricorn transits affect your 2nd house of money. By Yule Mars will be in Aries and domestic tensions will lessen. Decorate for the solstice with exceptional candles and a variety of lights. A child involves you in sports or other activities.

January 1–13 Mercury will complete a retrograde in the late degrees of your sign. A new perspective on how to apply your educational background may develop, or you may come to terms with long standing concerns. Throughout the rest of January until Candlemas Mars will add zest and fire to your 5th house of love. A romance will be ardent and exciting. Enjoy the moment. Be philosophical if February brings a sudden change of heart. Break work into small segments and take frequent breaks during February. Your 3rd house has some combined aspects which will bring you a short attention span. Love will make a recovery just after Valentine's Day when Venus will be in Aries. Matters of the heart will be back on track through early March. Winter ends with many exciting plans for the future. Mercury will trine Pluto, widening your range of options. A favorable Mercury–Neptune aspect hints that a dream can bring valuable insight on the eve before the equinox.

HEALTH

With sensual Taurus ruling your 6th house of health, overcoming indulgences and addictions can play a role in wellness. Your habits, for better or worse, will be a key factor. From January through the winter's end, your ruler Jupiter will be retrograde in health-conscious Virgo. Correct any problems then to remain well in years to come. Past life or karmic situations, including your family health history, can be factors to study on your route to wellness.

LOVE

The May 30 Gemini eclipse in your 7th house of partnerships can mark a change in commitments. You enjoy a challenge in love, for Mars is your passion planet. A free spirited or unavailable type of person will captivate you. From late July through September, while Mars is retrograde in watery Pisces, matters of the heart can be complex and frustrating. Be patient, for the autumn season's holidays and early 2004 promise better times. Attend a horse show or walk your dog if lonely. A new companion could come along with your animal friend acting as a matchmaker.

SPIRITUALITY

Springtime through the end of August should be a cycle of great spiritual awakening. Jupiter, your ruler, will transit your 9th house of the higher mind in your brother fire sign of Leo. Magnificent outdoor panoramas or places of sacred tradition provide a catalyst for deeper insights into life's meanings for you. Meditate at an archaeological site where ceremonies might have taken place long ago. Lammas marks the high point in this trend.

FINANCE

The influence of others may have led you to overextend in the past. Two of the eclipses this year (May 15 and November 8) impact your money houses. Prepare for some surprises; stay on top of changes affecting your industry or profession as a whole. Your financial priorities are entering a new phase. With Jupiter moving into Virgo at the end of August it's important to develop and adhere to a budget. This transit will square your Sun and indicates that you must be realistic concerning what is affordable. Repair and rejuvenate what you have on hand. "Less is more" is a good guideline for financial planning at present.

CAPRICORN

The year ahead for those born under the sign of the Goat
December 22–January 20

Challenged by being born during the bleak winter months, your sign grows up to be the most durable and strong in the entire zodiac. Your character seldom accepts failure. Your endurance and persistence carry you toward success against formidable odds. You can be industrious, systematic, and practical, but you realize there is a deeper component to being truly successful. Unusual combinations of ideas and events can be instrumental in helping you reach important goals. Timing and synchronicities are a part of the path you follow.

You are anxious for spring this year. You have much to do. Powerful Mars transits your own sign until April 21. You will be motivated and assertive. Others will admire you and follow your example. Your mental prowess improves after April 5 when Mercury begins a long passage through Taurus, your sister earth sign. Your words or writings might win you a new love as your 5th house is involved. Choices you make through June 12 when the trend ends are going to be wise ones. Beltane, with the New Moon in Taurus, marks one of the most powerful times for magical workings you will experience all year. Prepare a ritual. Either romantic or financial success will come your way promptly. Health will be in your thoughts near the May 30 eclipse.

In early June Saturn, your ruling planet, will enter your opposing sign of Cancer for a passage of several years. A partner might need extra help and encouragement. Legal matters can be time-consuming and eventually disappoint, so pursue them with caution. Be helpful to others, yet retain a sense of detachment. Others may be reluctant or unable to return many favors. Your best opportunities for growth will come through your own efforts. Dedicate the Midsummer Eve sabbat to health, for Venus will be in your 6th house then promising strength and wellness.

During July several planetary transits in Cancer will join Saturn in your relationship sector. It will be easier to assess the roles others play and to work out obligations or projects involving them. You'll feel accepted and included. The Full Moon on July 13 in your sign provides insight and perspective. Others are more sensitive to your needs then. Transportation needs can be a focus as the summer continues for both Mars and Uranus will be in your 3rd house.

By Lammas Mercury will be in Virgo impacting your 9th house. Spiritual books, tapes, and lectures can be comforting. A business trip would be lucrative in early August. The end of the month finds Jupiter crossing into Virgo. This marks the onset of a very favorable cycle for financial security. If you've been considering getting more education in order to boost your income, now is the time to follow through. During September Mars and Mercury are both retrograde and oppose each other. Your 3rd and 9th houses, which link to travel, are involved. Transportation delays can be a bit challenging.

From the autumnal equinox through October 22 favorable transits from the Sun, Mercury, and Venus highlight career visibility and success. The retrograde pattern is over by then and your wheels are back, literally. By Halloween new friendships are developing, for there are nicely aspected Scorpio transits in your 11th house. Spend the holiday visiting a new coven or explaining the craft to interested outsiders. Expect a turning point in a love relationship near the eclipse of November 8, for it falls in your sector of love and romance. Listen carefully to what a loved one is saying at this time.

At the end of November Venus enters your sign where it will remain until Yule. This is a very joyful trend, accenting invitations and popularity. Your appearance is especially pleasing. The financial prospects are promising too. The New Moon on December 23 falls in Capricorn. It's a perfect time to prepare a list of goals and affirmations for your new birthday year ahead. January finds Mars in your home and family area. Allow a temperamental relative time and space to work on a problem. A home repair might be needed.

The last half of January through Candlemas finds Mercury coming to the rescue. It will move through Capricorn in trine to Jupiter. Discussion and analysis help; a problem is overcome and bright new ideas are plentiful. On February 9 Venus begins an almost month-long passage through your home and family sector. You will enjoy relaxing and entertaining at your house. Finding a new home or improving your existing one is favored. The last days of winter bring the love and passion indicators, Venus and Mars, together in Taurus, your 5th house of love. A really wonderful intimacy develops. A valued and cherished relationship becomes more stable.

HEALTH

Intellectual Mercury and Gemini rule your health house. Learning all you can about health situations is especially important. Retrograde Mercury cycles tend to bring important changes in your condition. The duality hinted at by the Twins shows that there might be multiple factors affecting your well-being. The May 30 eclipse in Gemini will bring important health factors to the fore. Your vitality will improve from late August on when Jupiter, the cosmic healer, moves into a favorable year-long trine to your Sun.

LOVE

Loyalty is very important to you, for possessive and affectionate Taurus rules your romance sector. It's important to recognize when a situation isn't working and let go, in order to make way for something better. Saturn's position in your partnership sector from June on can bring a close link to someone considerably older or younger. November's eclipse can bring a new cycle concerning love. The very end of the year, from mid to late March, should be truly wonderful for romance. Both Venus and Mars, god and goddess of passion and love, will smile on you.

SPIRITUALITY

Jupiter will begin a year-long passage through your spirituality sector when it enters Virgo at the end of August. Healing can play a key role in your spiritual path. This involves the link between the mind and body as well as natural remedies. Always prepare for rituals in advance and be certain about the details of ceremonies. The Virgo link favors efficiency and clarity. Propriety and a sense of the sacred will uplift your spirit.

FINANCE

Over the past few years the erratic Aquarius transits of Uranus and Neptune in your 2nd house of money have brought changing values. Overall, the year should bring improvements, for Uranus is moving on. There are some good combinations in the earth signs impacting you periodically throughout the year. Saturn's influence shows the need to be cautious about entering into binding business partnerships. Only lend money if you can afford to make it a gift. Double check all legal situations that might impact your finances and resolve these as quickly as possible with a minimal investment of time and other resources.

AQUARIUS

The year ahead for those born under the sign of the Water Bearer
January 21–February 19

Others see a hint of greatness in you because you find deep satisfaction in promoting peace and liberation for all. That which you give away is illustrated by the water which streams generously from the Water Bearer's jug. But Aquarius is an intellectual and imaginative air sign, not an emotion-charged water sign. So our Water Bearer stands apart from his gift. This illustrates the deepest truth about Aquarians. Preservation of individuality at all costs while doing good to others is vital to your happiness.

The last several years have been truly strange. Uranus, your ruler, has been making a once-in-84-years trek through your birth sign. Now Uranus exits, and you are ready to enjoy greater stability. Dreams can help you, for mystical Neptune will still be passing over your Sun all year. Your creativity is at a peak. This can be good or bad depending upon how you use it.

Love prospects are bright and beautiful as spring begins. Venus will be in your birth sign until March 27. Plan a celebration of the equinox with a cherished one. Early April brings some communication glitches, for Mercury and Jupiter in fixed signs make rough aspects. When Mars enters your birth sign on April 21 you'll have had enough. Your assertiveness will intensify under this transit. Much can be accomplished, although you will be surrounded by controversy through mid-June. Celebrate Beltane at home.

The New Moon on May 1 is in your house and family sector. The May 30 eclipse in Gemini highlights love and creativity. A new passion, for either a person or a creative project, can come into your life near that date. As Midsummer Day approaches Mercury, Venus, and the Sun activate the promise of the Gemini eclipse. A period of great happiness is created.

During July Mars joins Uranus in your 2nd house of finance. You will feel the urge to work harder and earn more. Prepare for an unexpected purchase or expense. Jupiter will complete an opposition to your Sun during July and August. A partner's judgment can be a bit off. Don't take financial advice from others. Verify claims and information. Cast spells for truth and clarity at Lammastide.

A Full Moon in your sign falls on August 12. It is strongly tinged by Neptune. Your hunches are very keen. Communication with the spirit world can be a spectacular success. An opposition from Venus brings some charming and gifted people your way through the 22nd or so. At the end of the month Jupiter changes signs and will begin to have an impact on finances and investments. The generosity of others, perhaps even in the form of an insurance settlement, will improve your quality of life over the next year. During September several retrograde planets are prominent, especially Uranus. Uranus will re-enter your birth sign for one final passage before moving permanently into Pisces in late December. You are reliving the final chapter of an old cycle. Enjoy all that is coming to an end now, knowing that soon there will be progress.

The autumnal equinox brings favorable influences to your 9th house. Art and literature that suggest spiritual growth or faraway places delight you. The trend continues through the first week of October. Your cheerful state of mind will draw companions from October 6-23 when Mercury trines your Sun. Your humor and charm will leave lasting impressions. This is a wonderful cycle to do writing for publication. The New Moon on October 25 impacts your career and recognition sector.

Through All Hallows other transits cross the same area. You will feel ambitious and anxious to show what you can do. Your image and reputation are enhanced. Do rituals to open doors and stimulate your talent.

Uranus, your ruler, will turn direct on November 8 under the lunar eclipse. You'll want to leave behind anything you've outgrown. New friends can be helpful, for Sagittarius planets will brighten your 11th house in November. A novel goal will become important near the time of the solar eclipse on November 23. During the weeks before Yuletide, finances demand attention. You'll work hard to acquire greater security. Suddenly the tension lessens when Venus enters your sign on December 21. A surprise windfall could come your way near that shortest day of the year. Your popularity will peak during the rest of December through January 13 as Venus continues to smile.

During the last half of January Mercury will slip into the 12th house. You will feel the need to keep secrets through Candlemas. Discretion is an issue. On January 21 the New Moon provides a perfect opportunity for self analysis and soul-searching. It will be easier to express yourself when Mercury changes signs after February 7. Travel prospects are most interesting throughout the rest of the month, especially near Valentine's Day.

Home and heritage can seem a little restrictive during February for there are a pair of Taurus transits in the 4th house. Your tastes and priorities aren't like those of relatives. Flexibility and patience help. After March 12 a neighbor becomes a better friend.

HEALTH

Your health is strongly linked to the Moon, for the sign of Cancer rules your health house. Observe how New and Full Moon days impact your vitality for several months. Use the Moon Calendar elsewhere in the Almanac to determine which Moon signs mark times when you feel stronger. Surroundings affect your health. Avoid people and places which make you feel unwell. The early days of spring favor starting an exercise program, as Mars in your sign then gives you added energy.

LOVE

This year's eclipse pattern in your 5th house of love promises some interesting social opportunities. A new relationship can begin suddenly in either May or November. You are growing disenchanted with someone who hasn't lived up to his or her promises, as Jupiter has been afflicted in your 7th house of partnership. By the end of August you will feel ready to move forward.

SPIRITUALITY

On April 16 the first Full Moon of the year will fall in your 9th house of philosophy and spirit. The four weeks following that lunation will bring a spiritual awakening. Sometimes the Water Bearer has been portrayed as an angel, indicating that your sign has an affinity with angels. Call upon one. A response will come, although it might not exactly be as you expected.

FINANCE

Mars makes a very long passage through your 2nd house of finances this year, from mid-June through mid-December. Uranus will hover near the cusp of that same area. This shows there can be some unexpected financial situations erupting. Prepare to work hard to acquire added security. Enjoy all that you have rather than lamenting what you lack. It's hard for you to admit this to yourself sometimes, but you are really quite materialistic. Pragmatic Saturn is your co-ruler. Money represents freedom and independence to you.

PISCES

*The year ahead for those
born under the sign of the Fish*
February 20–March 20

The Fish are joined by a silver cord which represents the link between the earthly and the heavenly realms. It's the thread which keeps the Fish figures together while they struggle forever to swim in opposite directions. That image holds a valuable key in analyzing those born under the water sign of Pisces. Pulling in the right direction is of the utmost importance if you are to live up to your highest potentials. Your ruler, Neptune, is the planet of poetry and visionary creativity, yet is also linked to deceit and curious chemical combinations.

Prepare for a thrilling year as Uranus enters your birth sign. The springtime sets the stage for a whole new cycle. Changes can occur quite suddenly, almost before you realize it. Devote the vernal equinox to a ritual for freshness. March 28–April 20 Venus will bring happiness as it moves rapidly through your birth sign. Others will admire and appreciate you. Your legendary charm is in top form. Put effort into solidifying a relationship.

By Beltane Taurus planets will be gathering in your 3rd house, including Mercury. Mercury will be retrograde for much of May. Exchange ideas; be a good listener. With your tendency to daydream, you could miss out on or misinterpret important details. The May 15 eclipse in Scorpio is very favorable for higher education and for travel plans. The May 30 eclipse will impact your home and family sector. There may be some coming and going within your home. An interesting fact linked to your genealogy could surface.

As June begins, Saturn will enter your 5th house, which is ruled by Cancer. The care of children can become a responsibility, but will still be satisfying. You could be drawn toward an avocation which requires a great investment of time, money, and energy but which will add much to your life. Your kindness to a loved one who needs support will add stability and meaning to the relationship. By the summer solstice Mars will be in your sign, remaining there until December 16. This is a very long passage and in many ways will set the tone for your entire year. You will become more motivated and assertive. Controversy will tend to surround you. Focus on constructive outlets for your energy. Water sports and dance can be therapeutic.

July should be a happy month, for both Venus and Mercury will move through Cancer to trine your Sun. The strong water sign emphasis will create a climate of ease and acceptance. Love trends are truly wonderful, for this pattern pivots in your 5th house of romance. At Lammas your health sector is bright with Jupiter and other Leo transits there. Spend time in the healing rays of the Sun. At the end of August Jupiter will enter Virgo, your opposing sign, where it will remain for an entire year. This shows a great deal of growth in relationships. A marriage or other partnership will be very nurturing. Legal matters should work out in your favor. The Full Moon of September 10 in your own sign of Pisces will reveal the specifics. That lunation is excellent for astral travel.

At the autumnal equinox, Uranus will temporarily leave your sign to retrograde back into Aquarius. Suddenly life is more stable and familiar. Changes are coming, but you need not worry about them just yet. Someone close to you has extra cash and could be quite generous as October begins. All Hallows finds Scorpio and Cancer transits harmonizing with you. Share the sabbat with a loved one. Spiritual awareness is high.

November can bring some interesting career developments. The Sagittarius eclipse on the 23rd is in your 10th house of fame and fortune. Pluto, Mercury, and Venus are all close to the eclipse path. A job could be ending. Don't try to struggle against the inevitable. If one door closes another will open. Update your job knowledge and skills.

December finds friends suggesting new goals and projects. Membership in an organization can prove invaluable. Capricorn transits sextile your Sun from the 11th house. This shows those who genuinely like you offering practical support. By Yule, more tranquillity than you've experienced in many months will be present. Mars will have left your sign at last.

Dedicate the winter solstice to celebrating peace, both in the world and within yourself. January begins with restless Uranus present in your sign. Diversify rather than getting bogged down by one large, overwhelming project. The month grows happier near the 15th when Venus enters Pisces. Finances brighten and your heart is warmed by the love and regard of others. Reach out to others; you will be warmly received. Mid-month Mercury and Neptune will hide in your 12th house. Your inner life will be especially active. The Pisces New Moon on February 20 brings you a deeper sense of self.

Mercury will move into Pisces near your birthday. A short journey is productive near then. Your memory and learning ability will be in top form. Saturn will complete a retrograde in your 5th house of love during the second week of March. A relationship that was on hold moves forward as winter wanes. A problem linked to child care suddenly dissolves.

HEALTH

Your health takes a turn for the better as the year begins, for Jupiter is in your health sector. Don't lapse into any negative dietary or lifestyle patterns though. From May 15–October 22 Neptune, your ruler, will be retrograde in your 12th house. Get enough rest then and avoid companions or situations which you know aren't good for you. Your long-term wellness depends upon you being your own best friend during this retrograde period.

LOVE

A stable and serious relationship based on mutual respect and commitment is truly possible this year. Saturn will enter your 5th house in early June and will be supported by a trine from Mars in Pisces through mid-December. Venus augments the good pattern in July and October when she too transits the water signs. There could be an age difference with one to whom you develop an attachment.

SPIRITUALITY

Allow others to share their spiritual experiences with you this year. Sociable Uranus is entering your birth sign, bringing opportunities for new contacts. Your perceptions can be broadened and changed by associates. Since Uranus has a special link to astrology, this trend hints that deeper studies of the stars can help your spirituality expand. Reflect upon your Chinese, Native American, and Celtic signs for deeper insight. A Vedic horoscope, the sacred astrology of India, could also be most helpful.

FINANCE

Jupiter, the wealth indicator, will make first a quincunx, then an opposition to your Sun this year. This shows that external factors will impact your security. The economy as a whole as well as choices made by others can be part of the pattern. Adapt. Become absorbed in doing that which you most enjoy. Pursue it and have faith that the money will follow. It will.

Walter Crane

Nighttime People in a Daytime World

There are those of us who prefer night to day, and an explanation for the preference may be simple and logical. If you sleep deeply, awake slowly, and only reach a high level of energy late in the day, you probably qualify as a night person. Then again, you may be a natural witch. Whatever the reason, rest assured the current workaday world views you with less than kindness, even contempt.

A night person usually hurries in late for work. The sacred hour of nine a.m., so significant to employers and fellow employees, holds dread for those whose spirit belongs to the night. The Monday to Friday routine begins with a fiendish alarm buzz, followed by a frantic preparation to face the street, interminable traffic delays, and an overwhelming expectation of failure. There's that disparaging glance from the receptionist, who appears to regard your tardiness as a personal affront. To make up the time you may work through lunch hour, skip a coffee break, stay late to no avail. The scales won't balance. Day people, clearly in the majority, are convinced your lack of punctuality cheats the system.

To change your habits, if you must, take practical measures. Convince yourself that time is relative. On weekends when hours don't matter, try sleeping and waking earlier. Figure out exactly how long you need before you're ready to join the rest of the population. Set your alarm clock accordingly and allow yourself enough time to reach that goal. There's so much happening at night. I don't want to go to bed early and miss it, you probably think. All right. Try sleeping less. You may only need seven hours to awake refreshed.

Why conform at all? Change jobs. Investigation will prove there are many employment opportunities for night people. An artist or writer can always freelance. Your existence may be more economically risky, but there are trade-offs. Your time is your own. You might consider starting your own business with an appropriate work schedule.

But should you enjoy your current occupation and the only troublesome aspect is the attitude of those around

Mathilde Ade

you, take a tip from the witch world. Refuse to be intimidated. Assume a nonchalant manner. Use your wits. Answer a question with a question. Keep in mind that by appearing crestfallen and offering excuses, you only invite condemnation.

Every dominating society has its rules. When those rules inhibit your activity and disturb your peace of mind, you must find ways to work around them. Perform your job well, become an invaluable source of skill, faithfully execute the tasks assigned. The Daytime Powers That Be may be smart enough to appreciate your efforts and forgive an habitual slow start. If not, move on.

Ghosts of the Dry Tortugas

Seventy miles from Florida's Key West lie a chain of seven small islands, lovely and mysterious, spanning a spectacular stretch of turquoise water and coral reefs. In 1513 Ponce de León discovered and named the islands the *Tortugas*, Spanish for the abounding tortoises. "Dry" was added on mariners' maps to warn sailors that the islands had no fresh water. Over the next five centuries the site became steeped in rich legends that embrace pirates, soldiers, war prisoners, and improbable dramatic entertainments. To add to the tales, such frequent apparitions appeared that sailors call the islands "The Seven Ghosts."

The spectral sightings closely tie in to the tumultuous history of the islands, now a national park. For three hundred years they were the hideouts of the most notorious pirates roving the Caribbean. The area got less freewheeling when our country took control of the area, shortly after Florida was ceded to the United States. Twenty years later, in 1846, the administration realized that controlling navigation in the Gulf of Mexico relied on buttressing the Tortugas. A fort was begun, a massive project that would take 30 years to complete. Fort Jefferson resembles a romantic medieval castle, 45 feet high, complete with a moat and drawbridge. The beautiful masonry forms elaborate arches, tiered halls, spiral staircases, three stories of residential quarters, a huge kitchen and a chapel. Eventually the fort housed 800 residents, and its archives offer pictures from early days detailing a handsome, prosperous community. Water was stored in cisterns and more was shipped from outside to hold in underground tanks.

The pleasant character of the fort changed abruptly during the Civil War, when the site became a Union prison. Graffiti over the door of a gunroom used as a dungeon says it all. "Thee who enter here leave hope behind," a paraphrase of the ominous portal to Hell from Dante's *Divine Comedy*, "All hope abandon ye who enter here." Adding to the misery of both inmates and soldiers, yellow fever struck out of nowhere; dysentery and scurvy also prevailed. During the 1860's, 86 per cent of the population was stricken.

What remained of the colony found an improbable answer to scurvy. They formed the Dry Tortugas Dramatic Club and performed successfully in Key West, raising enough money to buy limes and vegetables to combat the scurvy that sickened virtually all the soldiers and prisoners. The club offered a minstrel show, infantry band, acrobats and weight lifters.

As for the ghosts, appearances are so frequent that the park staff calls the site "Spook Central." One grave belongs to a Mrs. Lowe, the wife of one of the lighthouse keepers, and her wraith is often seen by visitors and staff. The spirit of Private Winters, who died after being shot in a lonely corridor, turns up regularly. A park ranger's wife reports seeing a Union soldier sitting on her bed removing his boots. The pet cat of the gift shop manager mysteriously avoids a certain staircase.

A journey to the Dry Tortugas offers an unforgettable experience, and travelers can reach the site by a ferry departing daily from Key West. The fort is wonderfully preserved and provides a fascinating glimpse into the history of the islands. They are a wondrous wildlife preserve, and snorkeling gear is available for visitors to view the colorful, magical realm of the sea creatures that abound in the shallow waters. For readers drawn to investigating supernatural phenomenon, the chances are excellent for experiencing a genuine contact with paranormal energies. You may even hear strains of music drifting faintly through the night, hinting that members of the Dramatic Club still perform for visitors willing to listen.

— DIKKI-JO MULLEN

HORSES OF MYTH

Long the subject of awe and admiration, horses often appear in mythology. Perhaps you know a steed worthy of a mythical name.

Helios, Greek sun god, drove a chariot drawn by eight snow-white horses.
Actaeon - brilliant radiance.
Aethon - fiery red.
Amethea - no loiterer.
Bronte - thunderer.
Erythreos - red producer.
Lampos - shining like a lamp.
Phlegon - the burning one.
Purocis - fiery hot.

Aurora, Roman goddess of dawn, was in charge of three steeds.
Abraxa - supreme one.
Eos - light of dawn.
Phaethon - the shining one.

Pluto, Roman ruler of the Underworld, guided four black stallions.
Abaster - away from the stars.
Abatos - the remote one.
Aeton - swift as an eagle.
Nonios - like no other.

Neptune, Roman god of the sea, struck his trident in the earth and created the first horse. His action produced some odd results.
Arion - warlike. A combination of human and equine characteristics.
Balios - swift. Sired by the west wind and born of a harpy.
Hippocampus - horse of the field. Head and forelegs of a horse, body and tail of a dolphin.

The heavenly twins, Castor and Pollux, owned two celebrated horses.
Cylleros - named for Cylla in Troas.
Harpagus - one that carries off rapidly.

Most renowned in classical myths, pride of the Olympian stables, is the magnificent winged stallion.
Pegasus - of the wells.

Norse mythology has its share of noble equines. The horse of Day:
Skinfaxi - shining-mane.
The horse of Night, from whose bit "rime-drops" fall and bedew earth.
Hrimfaxi - frost-mane.

Sun's chariot, driven by the maiden Sol, was drawn by
Aarvak - early waker.
Alsvid - all swift, drew the chariot of the Moon.

Odin, chief god of the Norse, rode a remarkable gray horse with eight legs that represented winds blowing from the eight principal points of the compass.
Sleipnir - sliding one.

Window on the Weather

The generally accepted notion that manmade global warming is a reality, a serious threat to the planet, may mask another surprising and alarming eventuality. Woods Hole Oceanographic Institute scientists theorize that natural or human-induced global warming during the past 30 years may have created a backlash that will actually lead to a pronounced cooling of the climate.

Fresh-water buildup from melting icecaps may be reaching critical levels from which an alternation of ocean currents will occur. Temperatures may drop over the next 10 years by 10 degrees Fahrenheit in the Northeast and by 5 degrees Fahrenheit throughout the rest of the U.S. – changes that may persist for hundreds of years. The greatest effects of this sea change would be experienced over North America and Europe, where 60 percent of the world's goods and services are created.

For over a decade, the interrelationship of other elements have been understood to regulate temperatures: volcanoes, the earth's outer crust, and the three states of water as liquid, ice and vapor. This latest revelation indicates how quickly a change in the integrated forces can drastically effect our climate in a global way.

— TOM C. LANG

SPRING

MARCH 2003. We can anticipate a slow recovery from last summer's drought, the hottest and driest since the Dust Bowl days of the thirties. The remnants of this winter's feeble El Niño will spur Gulf Coast and Southeast rainfall. Last year's subdued tornado levels will pick up. The southern Appalachians can expect a brief wet snowfall in north Georgia, east Tennessee and the western Carolinas. The Southwest receives more consistent rain and snowfall with a well-established storm system lasting several weeks. Energy from this storm will progress into the southern Great Plains with several tornado breaks possible. Temperatures are generally seasonable, although arctic air with wind and snow will surge through the northern Rockies. The Northeast is only occasionally windy and cold, although a mid-month Nor'easter threatens southern New England, with heavy snow possible.

APRIL 2003. Southern U.S. weather systems move slowly, allowing for some limited drought relief there. The possibility exists of an embedded thunderstorm containing an isolated tornado; keep a weather eye out throughout the south and lower Ohio Valley. An early spring snowfall is notable in the western New England mountains. The Great Lakes states remain dry for now, with farmers hoping for rainfall before summer. Southern California storms linger longer this year with the potential for mudslides. The Pacific Northwest is unusually dry and warm. Florida experiences several strong thunderstorms.

MAY 2003. Enjoy beautiful cloudless sunsets, a prelude to warmer, longer summer evenings. Temperatures reach summerlike levels across the midsection of the U.S. Haze and fog cover inner coastal harbors along the Atlantic and Pacific seaboards. Heaviest rainfalls are confined to the Carolinas and southern Appalachians. Expect sporadic rainfall in the mountains of the Southwest. Winter runoff is longer than usual in California's Sierra Nevada. Hikers get an early start in the Cascade and Olympic ranges of Washington State. Mount Rainier climbers should be alert to prolific late spring snowfalls. Temperatures are warmer than usual in the heartland. The Northeast and Intermountain West are a little cooler than usual.

SUMMER

JUNE 2003. On the heels of the weak El Niño episodes, weather systems are generally slow moving with wet weather lasting only a little longer than usual. Drought relief will be negligible throughout the Southeast, Great Lakes and West. Fire danger can rise rapidly, though reaching less than last year's severe levels. Wet weather becomes more common in the Northeast, with reservoirs filled to the brim and the corn crop set to return with vigor. Florida remains dry with afternoon thunderstorms confined to the interior.

JULY 2003. Notable this summer will be less intense heat in places where people suffered last year. In fact, pleasantly cool air will bring sunny skies and comfortable nights to the northern Rockies and Great Lakes. In the East, many days are hazy with spells of showers, especially in the Ohio Valley where clouds will hinder temperatures from reaching extreme levels. The Northeast is unusually wet and cool, with an eventful Nor'easter bringing wind and rain for a three-day stretch. Mariners should heed all warnings and stay in port when this storm threatens. Southern thunderstorms are slow moving and particularly strong within 30 miles of the coast and in the hills.

AUGUST 2003. The tropical weather season begins grudgingly. Last year's quiet pattern persists in the Atlantic Ocean, with a slew of named tropical storms unable to reach hurricane strength. One Gulf of Mexico disturbance will produce a drenching across the Southwest, a welcome occurrence for an area parched by a six-year drought. The Northeast enjoys incursions of cool Canadian air masses, bringing an end to a short spell of summer weather. A sharp cold front can produce a brief but newsworthy tornado in central New England. The Pacific hurricane season brings high surf to southern California beaches and monsoonal moisture from Arizona northward to Montana. Blistering afternoon heat is broken by violent thunderstorms on Florida's west coast.

What plant we in this appletree!
Fruits that swell in sunny June
And redden in the August noon.
— WILLIAM CULLEN BRYANT

AUTUMN

SEPTEMBER 2003. About five hurricanes will form this year, slightly below normal but more than last year. South Florida is again prone to a landfalling storm, as are Texas and Louisiana. Rainfall also spreads through the central Mississippi Valley and exits through New England and the mid-Atlantic. The jet stream pattern does not particularly support a hurricane threat in the Northeast this year. Snow arrives early in the northern Rockies, while the Southeast is unusually hot. Texas and the southern Great Plains feel temperatures in the nineties.

OCTOBER 2003. Though winter is still safely north of the border for most folks, brief incursions of frosty air chill the northern Rockies with snowfalls capping the higher peaks. Early snowfall is also likely in the New York Adirondacks and the Green Mountains and White Mountains in New England. A late hurricane, less than severe in intensity, brings some flooding to Texas. The weather turns quite dry for the rest of the country. Thule fog reduces visibility to perilous levels in the California Sacramento Valley; use your car's low-beam headlights for such conditions.

The trees are in their autumn beauty,
The woodland paths are dry,
Under the October twilight
The water mirrors a still sky.
— WILLIAM BUTLER YEATS

NOVEMBER 2003. The first cyclones of the cold-weather season thrash the Pacific Northwest and a fast-moving disturbance brings snowfall to coastal Maine early in the month. Lake effect snowfall returns to western New York. The jet stream pattern favors snowfall east of Cleveland and Buffalo. Southeast conditions remain tinder dry with high fire danger, and the California Santa Ana winds bring fire in their wake. In the southern Appalachians, abundant summer rainfall results in vivid fall foliage.

The world is tired, the year is old,
The fading leaves are glad to die.
The wind goes shivering with cold
Where the brown reeds are dry.
— SARA TEASDALE

WINTER

DECEMBER 2003. The solar energy output cycle that ended last year has reverberations this winter. More snowfall is likely in December throughout central New York State, Pennsylvania and West Virginia. Conversely, less than average snowfall is likely along coastal cities of the eastern Great Lakes. Early season snows change to rain from the mid-Atlantic States to New England. The Ohio Valley experiences an early chill, with below average temperatures and occasional snow flurries. The northern Rockies are powdered by numerous snowy days with blizzard conditions in Montana. Much of California is dry this month, while the Pacific Northwest is frequently stormy.

JANUARY 2004. Snow cover is sparse near the East Coast as many storms stay inland early in the month. Atlantic breezes will bring mild snow-melting air to the West. However, mountainous regions can expect above-normal snowfall from the north Georgia mountains to western Maine. Michigan receives unusually heavy snowfall and generally cloudy days. The Rockies enjoy sunny but cold days, and Denver enjoys occasional springlike days with balmy breezes from the southern Great Plains. Storm frequency picks up along the West Coast, and one particular storm brings 70 mph winds to the San Francisco Bay Area.

FEBRUARY 2004. Cyclones are generally stronger and slower moving as winter progresses. February has the potential to bring the deepest snowfall and strongest coastal winter storm winds. This year, snow returns to much of the East Coast. Bare ground until now turns white from Washington D.C., New York City and Long Island. The first of three February storms skirts south of New England. However, another storm with heavy snow and northeast gales sweeps eastern New England with a foot of snow. This third storm of the month is moderate, with general six-inch snowfalls from New York to Boston. Temperatures are below average across the Midwest and northern Great Plains. The West Coast experiences windswept rain and snowfall is heavy in the Sierra Nevada.

And now let us welcome the new year,
Full of things that have never been.
— RAINER MARIA RILKE

Edmund Dulac

MUSIC OF THE SPHERES

The theory of heavenly harmony originated with Pythagoras in the 6th century B.C. The Greek philosopher was an innovative genius in astronomy, mathematics, and music, a towering figure in intellectual history whose speculations still influence contemporary scientists.

Mathematics and music are closely akin. Both disciplines obey laws of the most exacting logic. Pythagoras believed that all things are numbers, and that numbers are elements of reality capable of expression through the rhythm, melody, and harmony of musical form. As he observed the night sky and the passage of the planets, it seemed as if the universe itself conformed to a particular order and pattern; so creating an unheard music which if perceived would prove to be of great value.

The concept was never lost. Two centuries later, Aristotle tried to explain why, if the theory was literally true, people were not able to hear the music of the spheres. These sounds, he wrote, have been with us since birth. We never have pure silence to contrast with them — just as a coppersmith "becomes by long habit indifferent to the din around him." Many more centuries would pass before another brilliant mystical mind would take up where Pythagoras left off.

Johannes Kepler, father of modern astronomy, was born in Germany in 1571. His grandmother had been burned at the stake for witchcraft. His mother at the age of 73 endured a lengthy imprisonment under the threat of torture on the same charge. Kepler, by then renowned and respected for having discovered the laws of planetary motion, finally succeeded in securing his mother's release. She survived the ordeal by only a few months, dying in 1622.

Kepler's unusual family background probably freed his mind from rigid dogma, and he firmly believed in the abstract theory of heavenly harmony advanced by Pythagoras. He was sure that if planetary movement could be understood in terms of mathematical ratio and translated into musical intervals, the puzzle of the music of the spheres would be solved.

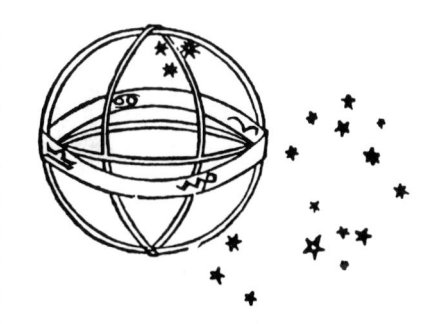

In Kepler's 1619 treatise, "De Harmonice Mundi," we find the musical themes he assigned to each of the planets known in his day. In the text below, Terra is Earth. The Latin notation followed by the symbol of the waxing moon reads: "Here is the moon's position."

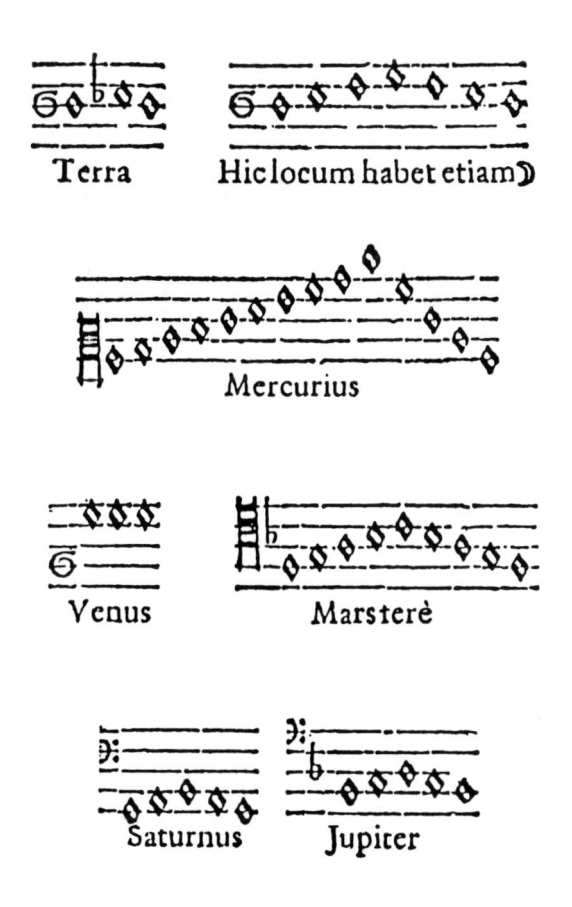

Terra

Hic locum habet etiam ☽

Mercurius

Venus

Marsterė

Saturnus

Jupiter

Now Blodeuwedd is an owl in the language of this present time, and for this reason is the owl hateful unto all birds. And even now the owl is called Blodeuwedd.

The Mabinogion from the Welsh of the Red Book of Hergest, translated by Lady Charlotte Guest.

THE OWL

THE BEHAVIOR of owls evokes dread. Their weird, melancholy call in an almost human voice shatters the still of the night. It may be followed by a bloodcurdling shriek or a sound resembling mirthless laughter. The owl, with hunting skill that rivals the hawk's, is a nocturnal bird of prey with extraordinary hearing and keen eyesight. Its soft plumage assures silent flight ending in a swift kill. Owls choose to live in dark forests, thick pine groves, and deserted ruins. You will never see a flock of owls, for these creatures prefer a solitary existence. Mobs of other birds, especially crows, are ever ready to attack owls. From time to time, owls must seek refuge in hollow trees, abandoned nests, or caves. If encountered by day an owl shows no fear and may appear tame to the human intruder. However, its watchful stare and cool manner implies equality. The meeting may awaken thoughts of lost souls damned to live on as creatures of darkness and evil.

Owls live in all parts of the world and sinister themes permeate their lore and myth. A compelling tale is found in *The Mabinogion*, Welsh legends of the early Celtic world collected from oral tradition and written down in medieval times. Arianrod, mother of Llew, declared that her son should "never have a wife of the race that now inhabits this earth." Gwydion and Math, powerful magicians and protectors of Llew, were angered by Arianrod's prohibition and determined to thwart her will. By charms and illusion, they conjured a wife for Llew out of flowers. With blossoms of oak, broom, and meadowsweet, they produced a maiden, "the fairest and most graceful that man ever saw." They named her Blodeuwedd.

Llew and his bride prospered until one day in Llew's absence a young hunter appeared at Blodeuwedd's door. As soon as their eyes met, passion filled their hearts. Ardently declaring their love, the couple spent the evening rejoicing in its wonder. "Nor did they hesitate to embrace — and that night passed locked in each other's arms." The adulterous pair plotted to kill Llew. But Llew led a charmed life and could be slain only by a bizarre set of circumstances. Blodeuwedd, by deceitful means, secured the knowledge needed to do away with her husband, informed her lover, and arranged for the murder to take place. When Gwydion learned of Llew's fate, he vowed vengeance. Confronting Blodeuwedd, Gwydion said, "I will not slay thee, but I will do unto thee worse than that. For I will turn thee into a bird; and because of the shame thou hast done unto Llew, thou shalt never show thy face in the light of day henceforth; and that through fear of all other birds. For it shall be their nature to attack thee, and to chase thee wheresoever they may find thee."

On a cheerier note: ancient Egyptians designed a beautifully stylized owl, the hieroglyph representing the prepositions *in*, *from*, *of*, *at* — which explains the owl's frequent appearance on tomb and temple walls. The Greeks, bless them, chose the owl as Athena's bird. The goddess of wisdom endowed the bird with her own noble aspects.

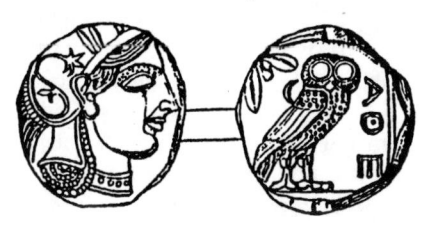

From *Magical Creatures* by Elizabeth Pepper and Barbara Stacy

ROMAN MERCURY

On the Ides of May, Romans might try in vain to purchase asparagus, necklaces or shoes, for on this day tradesmen shut up shop and gathered at the Temple of Mercury. They were paying tribute to the God of Commerce and the Market, Roman counterpart of the Greek Hermes. Of all the deities he was the trickiest and most glib; this fraud-loving god, generally depicted with a bulging purse, could sell you the Coliseum.

The holiday was celebrated annually on the anniversary of the temple's dedication in 495 B.C., following a great famine. The cult's founding merchants (*mercatores, mercuriales*) assumed, probably correctly, that a bit of smart trading could prevent starvation and promote prosperity — with a little help from a friend with divine clout.

The temple with its plebeian roots was modest, its annual celebration serving as both religious tribute and expression of guild solidarity, especially by corn merchants. Patricians looked down their elegant Roman noses at the cult, which they considered lowly, but that didn't seem to slow down its popularity. Altars, statues, murals and small roofed shrines to Mercury dotted busy urban intersections throughout Rome.

An excerpt from *Ancient Roman Holidays* by Barbara Stacy

MEDIEVAL MERCURY

The ancient god's spiritual significance diminished over time. Rome's commercial Mercury shares few attributes with his antecedents — Egypt's majestic Thoth and the divine Hermes of Greek conception. But certain elements of the god's original character were restored in medieval Europe. Mercury still holds a money pouch in one hand, but the other bears the caduceus, the magical staff of Hermes and emblem of the healing arts. He governs the zodiac signs of Gemini and Virgo, air and earth, and rules over an urban landscape. The primeval essence of eloquence, dexterity, and mental agility is illustrated by the variety of activities that flourish under mercurial influence. Study the woodcut on the facing page to discover the occupations ruled by Mercury.

MERCURY
Woodcut from *The Planets* (1470) depicts the various arts and crafts over which Mercury presides

MOON GARDENING

BY PHASE

Sow, transplant, bud and graft   *Plow, cultivate, weed and reap*

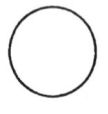

NEW	First Quarter	FULL	Last Quarter	NEW
Plant above-ground crops with outside seeds, flowering annuals.	Plant above-ground crops with inside seeds.		Plant root crops, bulbs, biennials, perennials.	Do not plant.

BY PLACE IN THE ZODIAC

Fruitful Signs

Cancer - Most favorable planting time for all leafy crops bearing fruit above ground. Prune to encourage growth in Cancer.

Scorpio - Second only to Cancer, a Scorpion Moon promises good germination and swift growth. In Scorpio, prune for bud development.

Pisces - Planting in the last of the Watery Triad is especially effective for root growth.

Taurus - The best time to plant root crops is when the Moon is in the sign of the Bull.

Capricorn - The Earthy Goat Moon promotes the growth of rhizomes, bulbs, roots, tubers and stalks. Prune now to strengthen branches.

Libra - Airy Libra may be the least beneficial of the Fruitful Signs, but is excellent for planting flowers and vines.

Barren Signs

Leo - Foremost of the Barren Signs, the Lion Moon is the best time to effectively destroy weeds and pests. Cultivate and till the soil.

Gemini - Harvest in the Airy Twins; gather herbs and roots. Reap when the Moon is in a sign of Air or Fire to assure best storage.

Virgo - Plow, cultivate, and control weeds and pests when the moon is in Virgo.

Sagittarius - Plow and cultivate the soil or harvest under the Archer Moon. Prune now to discourage growth.

Aquarius - This dry sign of Air is perfect for ground cultivation, reaping crops, gathering roots and herbs. It is a good time to destroy weeds and pests.

Aries - Cultivate, weed, and prune to lessen growth. Gather herbs and roots for storage.

Consult our Moon Calendar pages for phase and place in the zodiac circle. The Moon remains in a sign for about two-and-a-half days. Match your gardening activity to the day that follows the Moon's entry into that zodiac sign.

NAMES

Names are magic. A change of name is often a deciding factor between success and failure. A new personality of unsuspected verve and assurance may emerge when it is provided with its true name.

Perhaps your given name is a source of vague uneasiness to you. It is rather as if in a former life you bore another with which you feel strongly identified. Some, in a lightning flash of déjà vu, are fortunate enough to recall that name. Others continue to know the elusive feeling that the name they bear is not their own.

Here is a list of common given names from a century ago. We include their language source and original meaning. Perhaps one will awaken a slumbering memory.

A

Abigail (Hebrew) Daughter of joy.
Adelaide (Teutonic) Of noble rank.
Adolf (Teutonic) Noble wolf.
Agatha (Greek) Good; kind.
Agnes (Greek) Chaste; pure.
Albert (Teutonic) Nobly illustrious.
Alden (Anglo-Saxon) Old friend.
Alexander (Greek) A defender of men.
Alexis (Greek) Help.
Alfred (Anglo-Saxon) Elf in council.
Alicia (Greek) Truth.
Amanda (Latin) Worthy to be loved.
Ambrose (Greek) Immortal; divine.
Amy (Latin) Beloved.
Andrew (Greek) Strong; manly.
Anne (Hebrew) Grace.
Archibald (Teutonic) Nobly bold.
Arnold (Teutonic) Strong as an eagle.
Arthur (Welsh) Healer.
Aubrey (Teutonic) Elf ruler.
Augustus (Latin) Majestic.
Avis (Latin) Bird.

B

Baldwin (Teutonic) Courageous friend.
Barbara (Greek) Foreign; strange.
Bartholomew (Aramaic) Warlike son.
Basil (Greek) Kingly; royal.
Beatrice (Latin) Making happy.
Benedict (Latin) Blessed.
Bernard (Teutonic) Bold as a bear.
Bertha (Teutonic) Bright.
Bertram (Teutonic) Bright raven.
Blanche (Teutonic) White.
Bridget (Irish) Strength.
Bruno (Teutonic) Brown.

C

Caleb (Hebrew) Dog.
Camilla (Latin) Attendant at a sacrifice.
Candida (Latin) Shining white.
Carmen (Spanish) Song.
Cecil (Latin) Dim-sighted.
Charissa (Greek) Grace.
Charles (Teutonic) Strong; manly.
Christopher (Greek) Christ-bearer.
Clara (Latin) Illustrious; bright.
Claude (Latin) Lame.
Clement (Latin) Mild; merciful.
Conrad (Teutonic) Bold counselor.
Constance (Latin) Firmness.
Consuelo (Spanish) Consolation.
Corinna (Greek) Maiden.
Curtis (Old French) Courteous.
Cyril (Greek) Lordly.

D

Daniel (Hebrew) God is my judge.
Daphne (Greek) Laurel.
Darius (Persian) Possessing wealth.
David (Hebrew) Beloved.
Deborah (Hebrew) A bee.
Dexter (Latin) On the right hand.
Diana (Latin) For the goddess.
Dolores (Spanish) Sorrows.
Dominic (Latin) Belonging to the lord.
Donald (Gaelic) World ruler.
Dorcas (Greek) A gazelle.

Dorothy (Greek) Gift of god.
Dulcie (Latin) Charming; dear.
Duncan (Gaelic) Brown warrior.

E

Earl (Anglo-Saxon) Man; noble.
Edith (Anglo-Saxon) Pleasure.
Edna (Hebrew) Rejuvenation.
Edward (Anglo-Saxon) Guardian of property.
Eli (Hebrew) High.
Elizabeth (Hebrew) Worshipper of God.
Elmer (Anglo-Saxon) Noble and famous.
Elva (Teutonic) Elf.
Enoch (Hebrew) Dedicated.
Ethan (Hebrew) Firmness; strength.
Ethel (Anglo-Saxon) Noble.
Eudora (Greek) Generous.
Eunice (Latin) Happy victory.
Eve (Hebrew) Life.
Ezra (Hebrew) Help.

F

Felicia (Latin) Happiness.
Felix (Latin) Happy; prosperous.
Fiona (Celtic) White.
Florence (Latin) Prosperity; bloom.
Francis (Teutonic) Free.
Franklin (Middle-English) A freeman.
Frederick (Teutonic) Good counselor.
Frieda (Germanic) Peace.

G

Gabriel (Hebrew) Man of God.
George (Greek) A husbandman.
Gerald (Teutonic) Spear wielder.
Gideon (Hebrew) A feller of trees.
Gilbert (Teutonic) Bright wish.
Giles (Old French) A kid.
Godfrey (Teutonic) Peace of God.
Grace (Latin) Favor.
Gregory (Greek) Vigilant.
Guy (Teutonic) A leader.

H

Harold (Anglo-Saxon) Army leader.
Hedda (Germanic) War.
Hedwig (Germanic) Strife.
Helga (Teutonic) Holy.
Henry (Teutonic) Chief of a house.
Herbert (Teutonic) Glory of the army.
Herman (Teutonic) A warrior.

Hepzibah (Hebrew) My delight.
Hilary (Latin) Cheerful; merry.
Hilda (Anglo-Saxon) Battle maiden.
Hiram (Phoenician) Most noble.
Honora (Latin) Honorable.
Hortense (French) A lady gardener.
Hugh (Teutonic) Mind.
Hugo (Latin) Spirit; soul.

I

Ira (Hebrew) Watchful.
Iris (Greek) Rainbow.
Isadora (Greek) Gift of Isis.
Isaac (Hebrew) Laughter.

J

Jason (Greek) A healer.
Jeremiah (Hebrew) Exalted of the Lord.
Jerome (Greek) Bearing a holy name.
John (Hebrew) God is gracious.
Jonah (Hebrew) A dove.
Jonathan (Hebrew) God has given.
Joseph (Hebrew) He shall add.
Joshua (Hebrew) God of salvation.
Judith (Hebrew) Praised.
Julius (Greek) Soft-haired.
Justin (Latin) Just.

K

Kenneth (Gaelic) A leader; commander.
Kore (Greek) For the goddess.

L

Lars (Etruscan) Lord.
Laura (Latin) Laurel.
Leila (Aramaic) Dark as night.
Leo (Latin) Lion.
Leonard (Greek) Strong as a lion.
Leopold (Teutonic) Bold for the people.
Leroy (Old French) Royal.
Letitia (Latin) Happiness.
Linda (Spanish) Lovely.
Linus (Greek) Flaxen-haired.
Louis (Teutonic) Famous warrior.
Lovell (Old English) Beloved.
Lucius (Latin) Light.
Luther (Germanic) Illustrious warrior.
Lydia (Greek) Native of Lydia.

M

Malcolm (Gaelic) Servant of Columba.
Margaret (Greek) A pearl.

Martha (Aramaic) Lady; mistress.
Martin (Latin) Warlike.
Marvin (Teutonic) Sea friend.
Matilda (Teutonic) Mighty battle maid.
Matthew (Hebrew) Gift of Jehovah.
Maurice (Latin) Moorish; dark-colored.
Melanie (Greek) Black.
Melissa (Greek) Bee.
Mercedes (Spanish) Mercies.
Michael (Hebrew) Who is like God?
Miranda (Latin) Admirable.
Morgan (Welsh) A dweller on the sea.
Murdoch (Celtic) Sea man.

N
Nadine (French-Russian) Hope.
Naomi (Hebrew) My sweetness.
Nathan (Hebrew) Gift.
Neil (Gaelic) Courageous.
Nicholas (Greek) Of a victorious army.
Noah (Hebrew) Rest; comfort.
Norman (Scandinavian) Norse man.

O
Octavia (Latin) The eighth born.
Olivia (Latin) An olive.
Oscar (Gaelic) Bounding warrior.
Oswald (Anglo-Saxon) Power of God.

P
Patrick (Latin) Noble; a patrician.
Paul (Latin) Little.
Penelope (Greek) A weaver.
Perry (Anglo-Saxon) Pear tree.
Philip (Greek) A lover of horses.
Phoebe (Greek) Shining.
Phyllis (Greek) A green bough.

Q
Quentin (Latin) The fifth born.

R
Rachel (Hebrew) A ewe.
Raphael (Hebrew) God hath healed.
Raymond (Teutonic) Wise protection.
Regina (Latin) Queen.
Reuben (Hebrew) Behold, a son!
Rhoda (Greek) A rose.
Richard (Teutonic) Strong ruler.
Robert (Teutonic) Bright in fame.
Roderick (Teutonic) Rich in fame.
Roger (Teutonic) Famous with the spear.
Roland (Teutonic) Fame of the land.
Ronald (Old Norse) Strong ruler.
Rufus (Latin) Red-haired.

S
Sabrina (Latin) A Sabine woman.
Salome (Hebrew) Peace.
Samuel (Hebrew) His name is El.
Sarah (Hebrew) A princess.
Seth (Hebrew) Appointed.
Sibyl (Greek) Prophetess.
Silvester (Latin) Rustic.
Sophia (Greek) Wisdom.
Stella (Latin) Star.
Stephen (Greek) Crown.
Susan (Hebrew) A lily.

T
Tabitha (Aramaic) A gazelle.
Thalia (Greek) Blooming; luxuriant.
Thea (Greek) Goddess.
Theodore (Greek) Gift of gods.
Thomas (Hebrew) A twin.
Thirza (Hebrew) Pleasantness.
Thurston (Scandinavian) Thor's stone.
Timothy (Greek) Honoring gods.
Tobias (Hebrew) The Lord is my good.

U
Ulysses (Greek) A hater.
Una (Latin) One.
Urania (Greek) Heavenly.
Urban (Latin) Of the city; courteous.
Ursula (Latin) She-bear.

V
Valentine (Latin) Strong; powerful.
Vera (Latin) True.
Victoria (Latin) Victory.
Vincent (Latin) Conquering.
Vivian (Old French) Full of life.

W
Walter (Teutonic) Ruling the host.
Wilfred (Teutonic) Desirous of peace.
William (Teutonic) Resolute helmet.
Winifred (Anglo-Saxon) Win-peace.

Z
Zachary (Hebrew) Remembered of Jehovah.
Zadok (Hebrew) Just.

From *Witches' All*, A treasury from early editions of *The Witches' Almanac*.

New from The Witches' Almanac

A Classic Collection

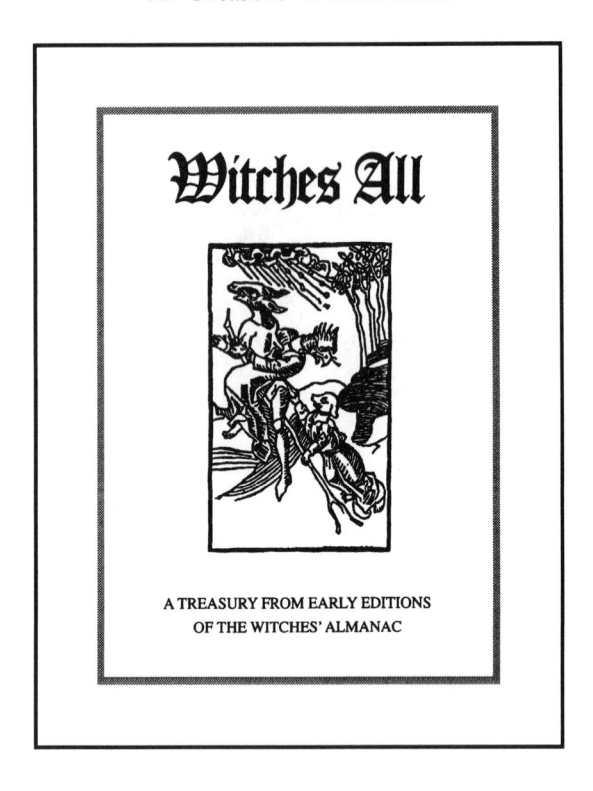

𝖂𝖎𝖙𝖈𝖍𝖊𝖘 𝕬𝖑𝖑

A TREASURY FROM EARLY EDITIONS
OF THE WITCHES' ALMANAC

Publication Date: Summer Solstice, 2003

Derived from past issues of *The Witches' Almanac*, *Witches All* will fill you in on more occult secrets than you can wave a wand at. This magical collection features a glossary of witches' terms, a collection of original spells from a 19th-century book of shadows, an occult alphabet, festival recipes, astrological lore and much more. A perfect introduction to witchcraft and a valuable addition to the library of a witch.

$13.95 • 112 pages

THE WITCHES' QUARTERLY

This quarterly newsletter appears at each change of season: the vernal equinox, summer solstice, the autumnal equinox, and winter solstice. Each issue boasts a myriad of special features including myths, useful information about plants and animals, astrology, and rituals and lore to help celebrate the passing seasons. Available by subscription. 12 pages. Mailed in a discreet envelope.

Subscription rates:
1/2 year (two seasons) $16.00
1 year (four seasons) $28.00

To order: Send your name and address along with a check or money order payable in U.S. funds to: Witchery Company, PO Box 296, Tiverton, RI 02878

...other titles from The Witches' Almanac

MAGIC SPELLS AND INCANTATIONS

Words have magic power. Spells and incantations, spoken or sung, have ever been a part of mystic ritual. From ancient Egypt to the present, those who practice the art of enchantment have drawn inspiration from a treasury of thoughts and themes passed down through the ages. This is a book of wonder assembled from many traditions used to divine the future, assure protection, find love, or make a wish come true.

MAGICAL CREATURES

Mystic tradition grants pride of place to many members of the animal kingdom. Some share our life. Others live wild and free. Still others never lived at all, springing instead from the power of human imagination. *Magical Creatures* collects their tales and tributes from earliest times to the present.

For ordering information, turn the page.

MAGIC CHARMS FROM A TO Z
A treasury of amulets, talismans, fetishes and other lucky objects compiled by the staff of *The Witches' Almanac*. An invaluable guide for all who respond to the call of mystery and enchantment.

ANCIENT ROMAN HOLIDAYS
The glory that was Rome awaits you in Barbara Stacy's classic presentation of a festive year in pagan times. Here are the gods and goddesses as the Romans conceived them, accompanied by the annual rites performed in their worship. Scholarly, light-hearted—a rare combination.

LOVE FEASTS
Creating meals to share with the one you love can be a sacred ceremony in itself. With the witch in mind, culinary adept Christine Fox offers magical menus and recipes for every month in the year.

MOON LORE
As both the largest and the brightest object in the night sky, and the only one to appear in phases, the Moon has been a rich source of myth for as long as there have been myth-makers.

Elizabeth Pepper's *Moon Lore* is a compendium of lunar tales, charms, chants, and curses from ancient time to the present.

A BOOK OF DAYS
A delightful book for friends of all ages. Here are 1700 gemlike quotations dealing with all aspects of human life, drawn from every source imaginable—from earliest records to the present, from Aristotle to Thurber. Quotations begin with Spring and Youth, then to Summer and Maturity, on to Autumn and Harvest, then Winter and Rest. Illustrated with over 200 medieval woodcuts.

RANDOM RECOLLECTIONS Vol's. I, II, III, IV
Pages culled from the original (no longer available) issues of *The Witches' Almanac,* published annually throughout the 1970's, are now available in a series of tasteful booklets. A treasure for those who missed us the first time around; keepsakes for those who remember.

CELTIC TREE MAGIC
Robert Graves in *The White Goddess* writes of the significance of trees in the old Celtic lore. *Celtic Tree Magic* is an investigation of the sacred trees in the remarkable Beth-Luis-Nion alphabet; their role in folklore, poetry, and mysticism. Richly illustrated as you've come to expect from our publications.

LOVE CHARMS
Love has many forms, many aspects. Ceremonies performed in witchcraft celebrate the joy and the blessings of love. This is the theme of Elizabeth Pepper's *Love Charms*. It's a collection of love charms to use now and ever after.

Order Form

Each edition of *The Witches' Almanac* is a unique journey through the classic stylings of Elizabeth Pepper and John Wilcock. Limited numbers of previous years' editions are available.

____2003 - 2004 The Witches' Almanac @ $8.95_____

____2002 - 2003 The Witches' Almanac @ $7.95_____

____2001 - 2002 The Witches' Almanac @ $7.95_____

____2000 - 2001 The Witches' Almanac @ $7.95_____

____1999 - 2000 The Witches' Almanac @ $7.95_____

____1998 - 1999 The Witches' Almanac @ $6.95_____

____1997 - 1998 The Witches' Almanac @ $6.95_____

____1996 - 1997 The Witches' Almanac @ $6.95_____

____1995 - 1996 The Witches' Almanac @ $6.95_____

____1994 - 1995 The Witches' Almanac @ $5.95_____

____1993 - 1994 The Witches' Almanac @ $5.95_____

____Celtic Tree Magic @ $6.95_____

____Love Charms @ $6.95_____

____Random Recollection I @ $3.95_____

____Random Recollection II @ $3.95_____

____Random Recollection III @ $3.95_____

____Random Recollection IV @ $3.95_____

____A Book of Days @ $15.95_____

____Moon Lore @ $7.95_____

____Love Feasts @ $6.95_____

____Ancient Roman Holidays @ $6.95_____

____Magic Charms from A to Z @ $12.95_____

____Magical Creatures @ $12.95_____

____Magic Spells and Incantations @ $12.95_____

____Witches' All @ $13.95_____

*Subtotal*_____

*Shipping & handling*_____

*Sales tax (RI orders only)*_____

*Total*_____

Shipping and handling charges:
One book: $3.00
each additional book add $1.00

Send your name and address along with a check or money order payable in U. S. funds to: The Witches' Almanac Mail Order Dept., PO Box 289, Tiverton, RI 02878-0289

Witchery

A CATALOG

A collection of hard-to-find quality items sure to be of interest to the serious practitioner. To obtain your copy of this full-color catalog, send $2 along with your name and address to: *Witchery*, Post Office Box 296, Tiverton, Rhode Island 02878

or visit us online at:
www.witcherycatalog.com

TO: The Witches' Almanac, P.O. Box 289, Tiverton, RI, 02878-0289

Name_____

Address_____

City_____ State_____ Zip_____

E-mail_____

WITCHCRAFT being by nature one of the secretive arts it may not be as easy to find us next year. If you'd like to make sure we know where *you* are, why don't you send us your name & address? You'll certainly hear from us.